Using a unique visual approach, yoga a
artist, architect, teacher, and author Micнael
you to shift your perspective, open your mind and empower tne
authentic YOU. Whoever, wherever, and whatever you do, you
can be free to Be different and Do differently in the world.

Drawing on his teaching experience of many decades, Timpson
explains that infinite potential and capacity for happiness and
creative fulfillment is already wired into every life moment. All
that is required to access this potential is change the way you
process and perceive experience.

Meditation sometimes seems too esoteric or separate from us
and our lives. In fact, meditation is nothing more than waking
up to life, as it is designed to be, flowing through the core of
everyone. In this easy-to-follow, practical teaching, Michael
Timpson expertly guides you into changing your world from the
inside out. The secret of meditation is that positive change is
not down to anybody else. You don't need to wait for the world
to magically change to be who you want to be.

You already have all the power and tools to create a new world
right here, right now.

Rather than waiting for things to change, Timpson empowers
you to harness the power of change from within, offering a
roadmap to create a new reality. The key lies in altering the way
you process and perceive your experiences, a skill he expertly
imparts through accessible teachings.

Mick will always be my favourite teacher. I will always remember Mick asking in my first class in 2019: 'Are you shaping your situation or context, or is your situation or context shaping you?' Before I met Mick I was struggling with anxiety and panic attacks. But then Mick's coaching empowered me to change from the inside out. It was an absolute joy reading A Modern Way to Meditate as it beautifully illustrates and communicates Mick's way of teaching in a very accessible way. Mick describes the mechanics of Modern Meditation in a way that sticks. I have been practising the skills in this book for three years and experienced real transformation. This book will teach you to change your perspective: 'change how you observe the world, and the world changes'. You will learn to notice 'you have an inside and outside'. You will reconnect to your human BEING 'learning not to only Do but to Be as well'. You will find how only in the NOW (Mick refers to an intersection point, the node!) can you actually change anything. Mick will help you to make the unconscious, conscious. And he simply says we need to do three tasks 'observe, create and love'. That's why this will be one book I will continue to pick up again and again for whenever I need.

Becs Mansfield

beanddo trained Modern Meditation teacher

ENDORSEMENTS

This is a truly special book. Mick is a gifted truth teller who makes manageable, understandable chunks out of complex concepts. Most importantly, he makes the world accessible for everyone – and that's Mick's secret sauce!

Amelia Lee
beanddo trained Modern Meditation teacher

Through the guidance in Mick's book, I have sought to make my day a continuous meditation. When I achieve a flow state it reminds me of Zidane playing football, conscious, purposeful, but in slow motion. It's like I'm playing a different game. Reading this book is a meditation and Mick gives us the guidance and the essential tools to unlock our creative potential.

Ste Taylor, Design Director
beanddo collaborator and client

Meditation practice, in class or on your own, allows you to repeatedly step into the world as it really is and connect to an infinitely creative source and the knowing that you are part of it all. With practice our being is transformed, away from the self we push out to operate in the world constructed for us, to reveal the joy of the self that we are.

We've all been on courses but the true learning, the learning that sticks, happens when we start applying what we've learnt in a classroom, or online, in everyday life. So if you struggle to apply your meditation techniques in the maelstrom of everyday life, this book will unblock you. You will be given tools that feel intelligible, familiar, uncomplicated, to take your meditation practice into everything you do. You will be supported by Mick's knowledge of related theories in educational, spiritual, scientific, artistic and medical domains. Mostly though, you will benefit from the eloquent and succinct expression, of decades of Mick's experience, crystallised into a life-changing book. Don't wait to get started.

Mary Cunningham

beanddo yoga and meditation student

Mick's Modern Meditation techniques have not only made a huge difference to how I live my life and perceive the world, but also to my professional work as a teacher. I use the Four As every day in my teaching practice - as tools to facilitate effective learning and for myself and the way that I interact with my students. In addition, Modern Meditation techniques have helped my work as a performer and help to alleviate performance anxiety. The benefits are far-reaching handing YOU the power to make a change and really, really do work. Don't just take my word for it though, read this book and practice the techniques, then practice some more! This book is the result of a clever distillation of thousands of years of wisdom combined with tools for modern people. I'm so glad Mick has written it all down for everyone to benefit from.

Pippa Goss, specialist singing teacher, professional classical soprano

beanddo trained Modern Meditation teacher

Other books by MICHAEL TIMPSON

Making Happy Work.
*A beginners' guide to navigating
the modern work with meditation. 2018*

A Modern way to Meditate

For Chrysta.
A very modern yogi !
Keep up the good work.
Mark XXX
Feb 2024.

For Beth and Jake
The best of all Conscious Action.

A MODERN WAY TO MEDITATE
8 Shifts to a Life-Changing Practice

Michael Timpson

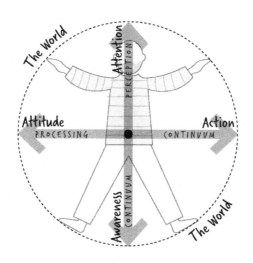

Meditation-based strategies to switch you on
and discover a whole new way of Being and Doing.

Foreword by Dr Anna Bergqvist
Afterword by Professor Fiona Measham

CONTENTS

List of Illustrations 1

Foreword by Dr Anna Bergqvist 4

INTRODUCTION
The Inner Architect 11

PART ONE:
A CHANGE OF PERSPECTIVE

1. The Answer is Within 31

2. The Possibilities are Infinite 54

3. Creative Action 61

4. Responding to your own Nature 72

5. Conscious Action 82

PART TWO:
CORE PRINCIPLES OF MODERN MEDITATION

6. Who are you? 93

7. Where are you? 101

8. When are you? 108

9. What are you? 115

PART THREE:
THE FOUR 'A'S OF MODERN MEDITATION

10. Strategies for developing conscious attention 127

11. Strategies for developing conscious awareness 144

12. Strategies for developing a conscious attitude 162

13. Strategies for developing conscious action 177

PART FOUR:
MODERN MEDITATION:
BRINGING IT ALL TOGETHER

14. Creating a whole new world 203

See the inferno 227

Afterword by Professor Fiona Measham.
What can we do with Modern Meditation? 230

Bibliography 236

Acknowledgements 240

About the Author 242

List of Illustrations

Figure 1   The mechanics of Modern Meditation practice.

Figure 2   A new model for 21st century life and work placing who you are at the core of what you do.

Figure 3   How the narrative of unconscious reactivity works.

Figure 4   Finding the still point.

Figure 5   What are you? A duality as a mix of two interconnected fields of experience.

Figure 6   How the two fields of experience appear as you in the world.

Figure 7   Where are You? Located where your sense of being and doing intersect.

Figure 8   When are You? Located in the here and now.

Figure 9   What are You? A matrix of attention, awareness attitude and action alive in the world.

Figure 10   Perception and Processing continuum.

Figure 11   Developing conscious attention.

Figure 12   Attention monetisation trigger.

Figure 13   Developing conscious awareness.

Figure 14   You are here.

Figure 15   Developing conscious attitude.

Figure 16 Night at the Bistro Californium
(Pop – Bang – Whizz), Mick Timpson, 2022.

Figure 17 Developing conscious action.

Figure 18 Preparing for Modern Meditation practice.

Figure 19 Avoiding obstacles to your practice – sinking.

Figure 20 Avoiding obstacles to your practice – drifting.

Figure 21 Avoiding obstacles to your practice – struggling.

Figure 22 Avoiding obstacles to your practice – attaching.

Figure 23 Example tracker – Emma's day at work.

Figure 24 Modern Meditation Daily practice tracker.

Meditation is simply the presence of awareness. It is not something you do but something you are. Awareness is the source and essence underneath your experiences, thoughts, feelings and all actions.

Modern Meditation is the process by which awareness becomes aware of itself as an unbounded, flowing, open field of potential underpinning everything. It is peace and happiness, and its nature is oneness, creativity and joy.

FOREWORD

Foreword by Dr Anna Bergqvist

'It was morning, and lo, now it is evening, and nothing memorable is accomplished.'

Henry David Thoreau, Walden; or, a Life in the Woods.

What does it mean to be or *intentionally embody* what Eckart Tolle famously refers to as 'the power of now'? Kabat-Zin's recall of an old *New Yorker* cartoon involving two Buddhist monks springs to mind, the younger one posing the same question to his older peer, who in turn responds: 'Nothing happens next. This is it.' [1]

Long-standing work in philosophy and psychology suggests we see our environment in terms of the actions that we can perform in it. All day your attention is directed outwards, navigating the world around you. We spend our active life in the world, responding to what needs doing. This is your lifeworld, your sense of personality and goals that drive you forward in achieving what matters to you and those around you. Throughout Michael Timpson's A Modern Way to Meditate, is a focus to retain that sense of purpose, to what needs doing in the first-personal mode of being "you" – but doing so by shifting perspective, using what he calls the four A's of modern meditation practice, Attention, Awareness, Attitude and Action, so attending to things as they really are, with acceptance rather than goal-directed projection.

At the heart of Michael Timpson's guide to meditation is a strong commitment to personal change 'from the inside out'

---

1. *Kabat-Zinn, 1994: 14.*

implicit both in the work of Thoreau and aspects of David Lynch's conception of consciousness as joyful and expansive creative awareness. [2] His own career as an architect, now artist and teacher, brings something new to the teaching and practice of 21st-century meditation practice. With over 30 years of study, teaching and practice, Timpson brings meditation into the everyday with his tracker led approach, combining reflective challenge of simultaneously trusting and questioning your own inbuilt skills (which become clear and empowered through practice) alongside the so-called 'Non-Doing Paradox' of practicing real yoga [3] as the two core features that guide Timpson's vision for relevant and effective meditation practice.

In concrete terms, what is required to fully be present to the power of Now is an engaged distance between yourself and your thoughts. In this way, if surprisingly at first, the role of the modern meditation teacher invites the well-worn phrase 'true happiness lies within'. It means taking the plunge into actively witnessing occurring subjective experience; to observe with enhanced Attention, Awareness, Attitude; and, most importantly, to trust what Action emerges in the moment, at its face-value without fear, doubt or intellectual apprehension.

Unlike both psychological and, conversely, psychotherapeutic analysis of experience, meditative inquiry into the messages from our lived somatic, affective and cognitive presence as embodied human consciousness requires immersive acceptance and patience with the relevant meditation object as they are in

---

2. See David Lynch (2006/2016: 27): "'When you "transcend" in Transcendental Meditation, you dive down into ocean of pure [vibrant] consciousness. You splash into it. And it's bliss. You can vibrate with this bliss. Experiencing pure consciousness enlivens it, expands it. It starts to unfold and grow."

3. Kabat-Zinn, 1994.

the moment for you. This sense of flowing wholeness or creative conscious action that Timpson describes is in my view all too often missing in various reductive or 'medicalised' versions of mindfulness as mere technique. [4] A Modern Way to Meditate presents us with a powerful alternative.

By itself, meditation does not confer immunity from patterns of looking elsewhere for answers in the continuous challenge that it takes to really be the person that is I in agency. Indeed, many people end up misusing teacher–led meditation retreats as that unhealthy 'momentary high' [5] rather than as an extended opportunity for inner growth and inspired, creative and conscious action that Timpson says is the point of practice. Precisely, because meditation allows a space for being and doing via your cognitions, Timpson's A Modern Way to Meditate affords the reader resources for adopting a true, clearer perspective on feelings and thoughts. The result is liberation from the fears and doubts that emerge in relating to yourself in terms of being who you really are and doing what you are really for.

Dr Anna Bergqvist

---

4. Compare the uses of mindfulness techniques for stress management and Cognitive Behavioral Therapeutic treatment of emotional dysregulation, for instance.

5. Kabat-Zinn, 1994.

'In all the activities of life, from the simplest physical activities to the highest intellectual and spiritual activities, our whole effort must be to get out of our own light.'

~Aldous Huxley. The Divine Within.

INTRODUCTION

The Inner Architect

When people ask me what I do, I tell them I'm an architect who teaches meditation. A mix that often provokes surprise and curiosity. 'How does that work?' they ask.

I reply, 'I work as an inner architect. Not so much from the outside these days, but from the inside. It's about helping people develop tools to change their world from the inside-out'

The practices I'll share in this book are how I do it.

Getting Here

My journey to teaching yoga and meditation in 1990 started when I stepped off a train at Charing Cross in London one January morning on the way to the office. As soon as my feet landed on the platform, I felt it. A surge of sickening anxiety shot up through my body. When it hit the crown of my head, it came with light-headedness. It was like a switch had been turned on. The dizziness didn't seem to pass. As I walked out of the station down Charing Cross Road to the office, this feeling stayed with me. It was like I wasn't there – floating and dislocated. Unable to hold on to where I was and what I was doing.

All morning, the feeling persisted. When I went out at lunchtime, I was breathless, tired and hot, and collapsed in a local shop.

It was my first anxiety attack, eventually leading to panic attacks, general anxiety disorder and depression. For a few months prior, I'd felt tired. My body, particularly my upper back, felt sore and sensitive as if it had been rubbed with sandpaper. I realise now that these areas of deep, unseen pain were like friction burns, resulting from me anxiously rubbing up against my mind and body, with others and the outside world. I had placed countless obstacles in my way because I thought I had to be different. I was in conflict with myself and the world, angry and frustrated, living a life of fear and dread fuelled by unrealistic expectations. Something had to change. If it wasn't going to be the world because that seemed very hard and painful to do, it had to be me first, the world second.

When I look back at that time now, I can see how my obsessions, fantasies, expectations, lost in a continuous rumination of thought in the way I did impacted how I was feeling and operating in the world. My default network which we will look at later, made up of interacting areas of the brain and nervous system, was becoming overheated as I continued to trap myself in self-centred thinking about the past and the future while also thinking about other people and what I thought they should and shouldn't be doing. Meanwhile, I had developed agoraphobia, which meant going outside was a mental disaster. Travelling 20 minutes on a train to Charing Cross from home was one of the most frightening experiences of my life. The tube was right out. My nervous system and senses were so over stimulated that sudden loud noises would make me almost black out. My office at the time was sympathetic and sent me home to rest. Of course through all of this, like most suffering from this state, the constant panic I felt on the inside hardly ever manifested on the outside because most of my energy was taken up trying to look and function normally.

It was exhausting. There would be plenty of occasions, going to meetings, presenting to clients, where on the outside I looked like a young capable architect while on the inside I was dying and fighting to breathe.

During the fear and pain however, there was something new in me that was coming through. Something deeper emerged that pointed to change. I found myself reading lots of Alan Watts, studying WuWei and listening to relaxation tapes. In 1988, I remember watching that ground-breaking documentary, The Power of Myth, in which Joseph Campbell, expertly interviewed by Bill Moyers, told us all that joy, bliss and creativity are inside, waiting to be uncovered. It was a huge moment for me, as it was for many.

As soon as I started yoga classes things started to change. Here was a system, a way of fine tuning my perception and directing attention away from what I thought I had to be, to who I actually was underneath all the pain and suffering. It was a process I could work with and understand and the impact was powerful. For the first time in a very-long time, I was me. I could feel my body not as heavy weight, full of tension, fear, expectation and stress but as an amazing flowing receptor of real experience. And I could see my mind not as a whirlpool of agitation and negative thoughts but as an expansive space of stillness and calm, full of possibilities.

After a while, a space opened up between me and my thoughts and feelings and, most importantly, actions. I realised my wellness, my happiness and truth were linked to going inwards, and as this happened, the outside world became brighter and happier. I could see more, feel more and do more from a place of purpose, creativity and insight. The anger and frustration were manageable and seen as what they really were - something I had made up. This, I realised, is how we change our experience of the world.

As I progressed in my yoga not only did I discover how to magically change my life, I soon felt inspired to teach and share it with others. I was already teaching architecture part-time at university. But, with yoga teaching there was a fundamental mental wellbeing, art and science process that everyone could use and become their own inner architect for change.

As I started teaching, I saw my students become free of the stress, anxiety and fear that had shaped their world. And, like my experience, in return, new vistas and landscapes opened up. New insights and possibilities arose from an unfolding, expansive sense of self and wellbeing. This, I thought, was how we change ourselves and the world itself.

When you teach, you discover almost everyone you meet and work with wants to change their world. Whether they know it or not, they are intuitively answering a deep call to transform beyond what they think they know or have been told. Everyone has the ability for awareness. Modern Meditation is the process by which awareness becomes aware of itself as an unbounded, flowing, open field of potential underpinning everything. As a teacher, that is the space I help others tap into. It's peace and happiness, and its nature is oneness, creativity and joy.

Go through this teaching with intention. It will work. It works for me, my students and my teachers, and it will work for you too. You'll notice, perhaps for the first time, you have unknowingly blocked off your innate joy and happiness. That's exactly what I discovered. I was getting in my own way purely because I had been told success in life had to be achieved in a particular way, from the outside in. So no matter your age or what you do, you can use these tools and techniques to upgrade how you see, feel, think and act to experience liberation. It's not too late to make your world anew from the inside out. You'll find out that knowing how to undertake what I call Conscious Action in the world will be exactly what you and the world needs.

Shifting Perception: No Effort Required

It's often assumed that meditation is some kind of mental or brain activity. Many say meditation isn't for me, 'I can't sit still. I can't empty my head'. Many think that meditation is about hard concentration, like focusing on a mantra, a candle flame or the breath. It feels like it requires effort and force, as if you are trying to resist or hold something. In fact, it's the opposite.

Meditation isn't an activity or training of the mind. Meditation is simply the presence of awareness. In other words, rather than assuming meditation isn't for you, it is YOU! Meditation is not something you do but something you are. So the only skill you ever need in meditation is shifting your perspective. This means that whether you are aware of it or not, awareness is happening now. It just is, constantly. Awareness is your essence, underneath all your experiences, thoughts, feelings and all actions.

Let's find out by shifting perspective right now:
For example, are you the one that is aware of your experience right now?

Of course, you are. You are the **one** that is aware of these words, what you're doing and where you are. You're aware of your thoughts and feelings, of bodily sensations, constantly changing, moving and flowing. You are the ever-present receiver, experiencer and knower of them.

The point is, are you trying to be that receiver of experience? Of course not. It's an effortless constant, flowing presence.

The next question is, could you be anything other than that receiver and knower of experience, now or in the past or future? Of course not – the awareness in you is you, moment by moment, which has been the same from the day you were born.

So far, so good.

Let's imagine that you could be separate and distinct from that knowing awareness and assume you are essentially made of passing thoughts and feelings instead. How would you do it?

You would attach and identify with these thoughts and feelings and, through no fault of your own, mistakenly believe they are you.

This is exactly where we are right now. When we attach to thoughts and assume they are the determining power shaping our experience, we block our pure Conscious Awareness. So instead of knowing that inner joy, we say, 'I am angry, anxious, stressed, lonely...' – all created in the mind and experienced in the body.

Thinking and emotions are, of course, not dangerous, but if you attach to them (think they are you), it distorts your perception and covers your innate ability to have Conscious Awareness. In turn, this creates a fake or illusory self, made of mental and emotional stuff that isn't you. That's why so many of us become lost or confused; we lose the ability to know and be aware of our true selves.

So it's easy these days, perhaps more than any other time in human history, to believe – I am this separate self, I am this body and this mind which is fundamentally me. **My wants, desires, fears, appearance and anger are the absolute measure of every other separate person on the planet and me.** This division and separateness put us on a collision course with the universe. We find that constantly and forcefully crashing up against the world, as I was doing, is the primary cause of unhappiness and pain.

This is when you might notice a void at the centre of your life. Many will unconsciously suffer this emptiness, assuming it's their lot, feeling unhappy and aimless, trying to seek happiness and purpose in the outside world of things, thoughts and feelings. But if you wake up to this situation, you'll probably want to find a solution. Turning to meditation, a new kind of searching shifts this Attention towards a deeper inwards reality.

A New Reality

So, this book is for...YOU

And everyone else.
And the planet.

We all come with a built-in sense of change. Some of us fear it, while others embrace it. We are wired for change, always on the cusp of transforming into something new. Otherwise, what would be the point? Change is constant in nature, and you and I are no different. But these days, that innate sense of change is simultaneously monetised, misdirected and controlled. Change is vilified and politically resisted from the outside by myths perpetuated by the media, politicians, leaders and society. No wonder we are feeling lost.

We all feel this need for change differently. It might be searching for more space or some confirmation about what you need to do next. You might feel stale, tired, pigeon-holed, overwhelmed or even burnt out. Looking around, you might feel like a visitor from a different planet – that was certainly my experience. It might be that more and more, you are saying to yourself, is this it?

Transformation is possible. In fact, it's happening right now, and here are two aspects to it:

First, meditation helps uncover a deeper presence of mind and body needed to fully engage in what you're doing to respond skilfully to the moment's needs. This, I refer to as your 'DOING' in the world.

Second, with meditation, we get in touch with a deeper, innate centre of consciousness, which enables us to live with greater energy, compassion, creativity and purpose. I refer to this as your 'BEING' in the world. Get Being and Doing working in unison, in the right way, and the world changes as you do.

Decide not to be held captive by those learned myths about what you do and how to live that stop you from being who you are.

> Get Being and Doing working in unison, in the right way, and the world changes as you do.

Let's start by breaking some myth making mindsets:

Myth 1 – I Don't Have Any Power

You already have all the power you need; seeking more is pointless. Cultivate a field of possibility around and in you because cynicism, scepticism and conservatism are exhausting and will stifle and close off all options. Be open to the power you have. **Modern Meditation will help you do that.**

Myth 2 – I Am So Isolated

You are never alone. We are all both locally and non-locally connected. Connected to everything. You and me, all of nature, everything is powered by the same source. It fuels your work and expression in the world like the trees, the stars and the bees. **Modern Meditation will help you do that.**

Myth 3 - I Just Don't Have Enough Time

You have all the time in the world. Forget speed and short-term expectations, and instead, open up to the now. Work where space and time are infinite and the only place to make real change. **Modern Meditation will help you do that.**

Myth 4 – I Need to Stay Ahead of the Competition

What for? There is no race. It's an illusion designed to control you. Instead, don't judge, don't make comparisons, and look for ways to be a generous collaborator with others and the world. Be open. There is real creative wisdom found in the most unlikely places. **Modern Meditation will help you do that.**

Myth 5 – I Feel Nothing Will Change

Change is constant everywhere. Seek it out, feel it and discover how to direct it and nurture a new web of connection, momentum and growth, inside and outside. **Modern Meditation will help you do that.**

DO IT NOW

Amazingly, meditation is the easiest and most natural thing because it's about Being and Doing the real you as you are right now. No matter your circumstances, you don't wait for things to change or for particular conditions to arise. Meditation can be done whether you are happy, stressed or sad. That's the whole point.

1. Find an upright chair and sit down. Take off your shoes and place your feet on the floor or a cushion. Sit tall and ease your lower back into the angle of the chair. If you can, position your upper back away from the backrest. Use a cushion behind your lower back if you need to.

2. Place your hands, palms upward, on your lap. Keep your knees pointing forwards. Slowly lower your eyelids or close your eyes. Keep your mouth closed and breathe through your nose naturally.

3. Now draw your attention to your fingers. Don't think about it; just do it. After a short time, you will find that your fingers respond to your focused attention. You will notice a gentle vibration inside the fingers. A sort of buzzing energy. This is normal.

4. As soon as you feel this sensation, try to maintain it. You will notice that to do this, it's all about your Attention. If you feel the sensation has stopped, it's only because your attention has drifted away. Bringing back the sensation in your fingers directs and reconnects your attention.

5. After a few moments, you will feel relaxed and a little more present. Just let this happen. You are discovering how to become deliberately aware.

6. Now, if you can, simply allow that awareness to grow. Just be aware of this growing awareness without judging or having any expectations. Just watch this awareness grow until you feel you are aware of the awareness. Your thinking mind will want to get involved and distract you. Instead, just pay Attention to how you are attending to the vibration. You will find you don't need your thinking, analysing mind to pay Attention or even experience what is happening.

We will look at this first practice in more depth later. However, if you feel something new or different, a little more calm, open and centred, you are on the path towards a profound shift.

A fragmented world.

Humanity is in pain. Even now, in the third decade of the 21st century, with so many advances in civilisation, humanity is suffering a deep crisis state – and it is self-inflicted. We are systematically switching ourselves off. We are the only species that seems to be knowingly engineering our unhappiness and perhaps even our demise. Our crisis is environmental, economic, humanitarian, political and cultural, created by our own actions and inaction, shaped by the way we have chosen to **see** ourselves and the world. Our perspective on who we are, what we do have to change fast. Perhaps then, if we accept that we suffer to know what the opposite could be, surely, we are at a turning point? There is no doubt a revolution of consciousness is happening as old mindsets and paradigms become obsolete.

I'm not alone in this realisation.

One of the reasons that prompted A Modern Way to Meditate was to help confirm in my own way the shift of awareness happening worldwide. It might not feel like it, but if we watch the world of I, Me and Mine, big corporations, unbalanced economies, self-serving politicians are crumbling. Since the banking crisis in 2008, and most likely much earlier, these aspects have led us to where we are now – inhabiting a living planet we have systematically exploited. All the natural systems that sustain us, including our connection to each other, are being broken for control and profit.

The result is that we are collectively making outcomes nobody ultimately needs. But there is a new intelligence of the Self, a deeper connected consciousness emerging, particularly in the young. I see it clearly in the design and yoga students I'm honoured to teach and work with. These amazing, creative people are having to tackle an ecologically, socially and spiritually fragmented world very different from the one I grew up in. On our current path we will eventually lose nature, society and the Self (yes with a large S). Modern meditation is designed to help address this in a straightforward way. When we reconnect to the last aspect – Self, we will naturally address the first two simultaneously.

An evolutionary jump is happening right here, right now. It seems, too, that it is voluntary – you have a choice. This time, it's nothing to do with the survival of the fittest, the development of opposable thumbs, tools, language or the discovery of fire. People are choosing to be awake. They are going inwards, not outwards, towards a more innate truth.

Many people are searching for a different way of Being and Doing. To become aware of something that cannot be seen but known and experienced beyond what politicians tell you and what the media insists is true.

They are discovering more than what we have been led to believe. The truth of the world and what yogis have taught for thousands of years – that underpinning everything we see, feel, think and do is an undeniable field of potential creative energy. An unlimited ocean of pure conscious intelligence that makes all sense perceptions, actions and ideas possible. That ocean is inseparable from who you are, and its essence is joy. Knowing this, intuitively results in awake individuals who may choose to live differently. All we have to do is know this and be sensitively aware of how the whole process works in you, others and the world.

To be fully alive to what is real.

Just Live

To do that, it seems that while you and I are here, we just have to accomplish three tasks; observe (pay close unconditional Attention), create (align with the momentum of change everywhere) and love (where the power to achieve the first two comes from).

That's it. Anything else is theory and mostly a source of confusion and pain. Knowing this is what Modern Meditation is for.

Meditation isn't elevated or opaque. It's simply a way of
seeing and responding clearly to what's in front of you.
You will discover that you are an opening, a portal through
which everything flows. To be fully alive, all you need to do is
collaborate with the flow.

This means growing towards an ever-increasing expression of
life as a joyous, conscious, creative, loving force of change. You
are part of the process. You **Being** here and **Doing** what you
do gives meaning. No matter what you think (and that is the
whole point). That is your only purpose. Your brain and nervous
system (the most complex processing machine in the universe,
as far as we know) have evolved to do just that – to run the
programme of life and living.

> The universe needs your
> participation to make it work.
> **You are creating.**

In short, you are a localised transceiver of pure flowing, whole
consciousness expressed through action and experience. You are
an instrument of awareness in and of the universe and how the
universe knows itself better. In fact, without you observing and
a conscious witness to the flow of experience as 'in-formation',
you could conclude that something was missing in that the
'universe would somehow be incomplete' [6]. The universe needs
your participation to make it work. **You are creating.**

6. David Storoy. 'David Bohm, Implicate Order and Holomovement'. Science & Non-Duality.com.
https://www.scienceandnonduality.com/article/david-bohm-implicate-order-and-holomovement

When Apollo 14 astronaut Ed Mitchel returned from the Moon in 1971, he reported what is often referred to as a samadhi [7] experience when he gazed at Earth from space:

'On the return trip home, gazing through 240,000 miles of space toward the stars and the planet from which I had come, I suddenly experienced the universe as intelligent, loving, harmonious.'

Meditation or Revolution?

He concluded that the universe is a flow of 'purposefulness – 'powered by love!' What a remarkable insight from a highly trained technician, looking through the small windows of his Command Module as it travelled back to the Earth at 3,000 miles an hour. Ed Mitchell's well-documented epiphany is common in astronauts and is often called the 'Overview Effect'. A deep state of transformation brought about by a profound cognitive shift in how we perceive and process experience. This shift in cognition is what I'm hoping you will discover through this modern way to meditate, but without having to fly to the moon and back.

---

7. Mahoney, E. 'Consciousness: Edgar Mitchell's Samadhi in Deep Space', Hinduism Today, 1 January 1, 2018. https://www.hinduismtoday.com/magazine/consciousness-edgarmitchells-samadhi-in-deep-space/

And here is what to expect:

Part I introduces some core principles of Modern Meditation, starting with what meditation is – a change of perspective in perceiving and processing the world. This is achieved by modifying and upgrading four key cognitions of Attention, Awareness, Attitude and Action. The four 'A's' are the core Modern Meditation skills.

Part II builds on the core principles and starts drilling into new insights that make effective meditation possible. Starting with questions about who, where, when and what you are.

Part III explores each of the four 'A's' to build and develop your Modern Meditation practice as a regular formal routine and also informally as you go about daily life. There is a strategy and guided meditation practice to make each A practice a conscious skill.

Part IV puts all of the above together into practical and effective everyday practice. There are two aspects to this application, 'laboratory' and 'fieldwork'. The first is expressed through a regular daily sitting practice. The second explores how to use Modern Meditation techniques in everyday life.

 To support you on this journey, you can download the online tracker by scanning the QR code here; this is a practical, interactive tool that supports meditation practice and Conscious Action.

Read this book to the end and surrender to its call to action and the invitation to form new outlooks and techniques. Along the way you'll find affirmations and journalling prompts that you can use to help this shift happen. Because a profound change of perspective, a shift in how we perceive and process the world, from where I'm sitting, is how we all survive. It can all be done with your feet firmly on planet Earth. And be prepared for change. Because when you discover **the four A's** on how to pay **Attention** via deeper **Awareness** cultivated by a shift in **Attitude**, the right **Action** will emerge.

It will happen. It has to.

Over the last 35 years I have taught, I have seen many students and fellow collaborators transform themselves and their world. They have learned this because, in their hearts, they know they need to embrace that inner momentum. To switch off old mindsets and switch themselves on fully. I have seen students begin to live their lives differently in a more fulfilling way and even change careers, change partners, and even change countries because they have discovered they don't need to believe what they've been told. They have discovered they already have their own tools to thrive.

These days might appear like the end of things, but that is the opportunity. There is still a chance to turn things around.

I'm looking at you here!

Meditation or revolution? Meditation is easier.

PART ONE
A CHANGE OF PERSPECTIVE

'The seat of the soul is where the inner world and the outer world meet. Where they overlap, it is in every point of the overlap.'

~ *Novalis*

Chapter 1

THE ANSWER IS WITHIN

'Out beyond ideas of wrongdoing and rightdoing, there is a field. I'll meet you there.'

Rumi

Lots of people ask, *how do I meditate?* The more helpful question to ask is, *what is meditation?*

The answer is simply a change of your perspective!

This means learning to look and then see differently from a place, which for many, will be a rediscovered location. Happily, you don't need to go anywhere to find that place because it's already **where YOU are.**

Using the practices, techniques and insights in this book, I will help you **look** at and **see** yourself and the world differently. I will help you reorientate inwards to look out onto the world. You will cultivate a different awareness, which will help you **observe, fully participate and shape** the flow of your life in the world. You won't be watching in a critical and judgemental way. It will be open and effortless, without attachment to any particular set of ideas, motives, concepts or pre-assumptions that you might have about yourself, others and the world around you. This will be a new and unconditional response from a place of freedom.

To know this freedom, you must dispense with expectation, assumptions and division. You have to shift away from what you expect of life towards what life expects of you. Forget wondering what the meaning of life is and instead **see** what life wants from you every moment. I am not suggesting not planning for a better world for others. My whole career as an architect and teacher has been just that. But your starting point should be yourself first, to **act consciously** first and thus get with the bigger programme.

For many, though, the bigger programme runs through life unnoticed. This is because we don't know it's there. We lack the skills to perceive and process what is really happening. This is because we are mostly held hostage by how we think, see, feel and act. We can either **unconsciously react to the world,** or we can **consciously act in the world**. There is a huge difference, and it's all down to fine-tuning your perspective. Modern Meditation is a process of self-observation.

> We can either unconsciously react to the world,
> or we can consciously act in the world.

Self-Observation: core principles

Using these practices, you will learn how to gradually know, define and distinguish between your everyday unconscious reaction and Conscious Action. Everything you do, no matter how simple, will be infused with flowing, playful, creative joy as you discover how to be a conscious collaborator with the world.

You will learn how to upgrade and empower four innate cognitions: **Attention, Awareness, Attitude** and **Action.** With careful guided practice and exploration, the result will be a direct experience of YOU as a centre of consciousness – a node point, a space through which your life is manifested, defined, shaped and flows.

A Modern Way to Meditate has brought together many of the experiences and insights I have collected and shaped over the years practising as an architect, artist, speaker, lecturer, yoga teacher and meditation coach. I've tried to keep it simple with an eye to making this ancient human practice relevant in a changing world.

There are three fundamental elements that underpin a modern way to meditate:

1. It's a framework for looking differently. If meditation is a simple change of perspective, then the first aim is to help modern meditation practitioners redirect attention. The intention is to recognise the blind spots caused by habitual thinking, which distorts attention, and open up to seeing a deeper reality of things and actions.

2. It's also a process for cultivating and implementing awareness-based change and growth by seeing ourselves in the world not as victims whirled around by fate, but as portals for creative potential and implementing conscious action.

3. It's a set of tools that, if used regularly, will open one up to help bring about deep evolutionary change by upgrading our mental, emotional and physical operating systems.

Change from the Inside Out

This shift of perspective promoted in modern meditation techniques upgrade perception so that we can see how action comes into the world and how the quality of our attention shapes its outcome. This, however, is our current problem because these days we rarely pay attention to anything for long. When we do, we often become attached to something that has been created to hook us and elicit an unconscious response – like most social media for example. We are distracted, completely unaware of the real source of all actions and ideas and that deeper inner consciousness from which we operate.

Human activity is constant but comes into the world via two filters – unconscious reactivity (habits) and conscious activity (creativity). Modern meditation as a process and practice provides tools to shift attention to that inner space of awareness that can distinguish between the unconscious and the conscious. This is the job of all of us if we want to cultivate and allow change and possibilities to flow. It's the difference between being asleep or awake. A narrative of evolutionary and societal change coming from so many young people but feared by those who can't adapt.

You Already Know What to Do: The Four A's

My Modern Meditation teaching uses four powerful interconnecting practises: **ATTENTION, AWARENESS, ATTITUDE** and **ACTION**.

The four A's help you rediscover a deeper state of awareness-shaped perception. The term rediscover: here is important. You have already come hard-wired with these skills. Over the years, you have unconsciously narrowed and distorted these skills from open, free-flowing creative perception to a distorted focus shaped by a lens of habitual thought, feelings and action.

Normally our capacity for Attention, Awareness, Attitude and Action goes unnoticed by the unconscious. We will be learning to flip this so becoming conscious tools – making the unconscious conscious. The practice is an invitation to show up to yourself, where you are, and what you are doing regularly.

The process is about establishing a consistent framework to support your meditation practice. It might seem strange to propose a framework or system when meditation is an open, flowing, liberating experience. However, in all of my creative work I have realised that it's the discipline of a framework that defines and shapes freedom. For a river to flow it needs gravity, banks, rocks and ledges.

Modern meditation revolves around four core skills that will shift methods of cognition and perception:

1. **Attention:** The power of directing attention on purpose, for purpose is key to all meditation practices. Modern meditation-based Attention practice is designed to strengthen one's ability for intention and resilience in a world which is otherwise currently designed to overwhelm. But it's a knowing sort of Attention that is needed. One which opens up a field of seeing that recognizes possibilities and opportunities as they emerge.

2. **Awareness:** Modern meditation then helps uncover this unfolding expanding Awareness. It's a place that has always been revealing that this deep experience is the real you – full of joy, potential and creativity, and not the one you think you are, full of want, expectation and prejudice. This Awareness shows you that you are a vehicle, a portal for change, and it comes with an open heart and mind.

3. **Attitude:** But the first two aspects of what I refer to as your vertical skills only emerge if you include your horizontal experience, too. This is you in the field of doing which modern meditation tools enable you to experience it as it really is. We shift to an Attitude that suspends judgement, labels and attachment. This opens us to a world of colour and beauty that already exists but is distorted via our partially blocked senses. This takes us to the world of the artist, a world beyond our limited compressed and biased viewpoints.

4. **Action:** We arrive at a new place in the world where what we do feels meaningful, purposeful, and real. This is where you

readily tap into your own sources of creativity, insight, and curiosity. It's where every Action you take has a rightness and authenticity to it. With practice, this new sense of flowing will expand, enabling you to hold space for others, too. This is what I mean by real leadership.

What I am keen to do is develop a meditation methodology to not only support individuals to shift perspective, but groups as well. It's possible to use these tools to help teams collectively upgrade and direct Attention in a way that focuses energy so that they can tap into a deeper collective Awareness towards what needs to be done. Using this insight in my career as an architect, I have seen how the quality of Awareness in people impacts on the quality of results. I have seen how groups of people working together can get it right the first time in what they are setting out to do because they are connected at a deeper level beyond ego, competition and procrastination.

You will discover that your success, purpose, creativity and joy depend on how you can upgrade and then turn your perception towards this space. A few people are lucky, unknowingly born with access to this inner capacity. However, everyone can discover it through Modern Meditation.

You can, if you choose, naturally grow happiness and wellbeing in life and design your world anew from the inside out. Because your unique opportunity lies in aligning with the deep source and uniqueness in every moment. We are all responsible for acting consciously, as we are invited to act according to purpose and destiny.

Life becomes concrete and meaningful when you learn to see, fine-tune and combine your dual aspects of **Being** and **Doing**. This way of observing, this new perspective on your **Being** and **Doing**, will provide you with new building blocks to create a different world.

Modern Meditation is designed to directly relate to everyday activities, not something separate. This is a Modern Way to Meditate. There are no mantras, special postures to master or breathing techniques to practise. I have already done all that for you through over 35 years of yoga and meditation teaching and practice. The process I have created here is simple, systematic, scientific, measurable and easy to apply, making it ideal for 21st-century individuals and organisations.

Making the World Work: Three-step Process

If there is one thing we know for real: the world is something we make, and it can be made, if we choose, to be very different. You might also intuitively know that somewhere in your life is the real and authentic, intelligent and creative version of YOU. It's always been there, waiting and wanting to be expressed, but until now has pretty much gone by undefined.

You might have guessed this already, but the world is NOT designed to make you happy. Don't wait for external things to happen or align with your *thinking* about what you need to be happy. But the real world IS designed to help you discover where happiness truly resides. As far as I know, happiness, creativity and joy are closely related to how you see and participate in the world.

It's an internal thing and a simple three-step process:

1. Get involved in the action, the doing of the world. It's
    constant and is happening through you and all around you.
    But take part selflessly. Work to help and support others
    always and never think about what's in it for you.

2. Undertaking step I reveals your real nature and identity. You
    begin to see who and what you are, what you are good at and
    what you are for. You are here to learn and grow.

3. Step II leads you to know that you are a vehicle, a conduit, an
    instrument through which love, creative potential, and joy
    flow into the world. So get out of the way – which brings us
    back to step I, where you work to keep the whole cycle going.
    The result is wellbeing and happiness for you and everyone
    else involved.

This all seems pretty simple, but the human world works
against it. These three aspects pretty much underpin all of the
world's wisdom traditions. But when you get it, you will know
what **beanddo** hero Joseph Campbell called following your 'bliss'.
You'll know it when that happens. All the above has to be done,
despite modern society doing its best to distract and compress
you. You won't find anything like these three stages on the
agenda of any business board meeting, even though I often
tried in my 'working' days. But in the end, these three things
fundamentally matter and will bring real success.

If meditation is the natural flow from being aware of being
aware to simply Awareness itself, then in terms of the practice
the framework indicates where each of the four skills define the

flow. You direct your *Attention* shaped by a particular Attitude to objects of experience. Then Awareness grows and you begin to be aware of Awareness, until you are Awareness itself – resting as boundless absolute consciousness – the source of all *Action*.

These four A's are a range of three-dimensional coordinates that you will use repeatedly to help you stay where you need to be. Working through the four A's, you'll learn to notice and unlearn habitual physical, emotional and mental tendencies that have held you back or pushed you off course. In many ways, you will defocus away from short-term distractions, let go and remember who you are. The objective is to break the illusion to return to a different space and moment, a field of experience where you know you are your true, authentic self. As we often say in our **beanddo** classes: *it's a place you will recognise because it's home.*

A different way of doing stuff

This is change from the inside out, where we learn to tune our attention to our inner self, our core being and the source of all actions and perceptions. Modern meditation allows us to sense this and knowingly connect to different, newer waves of potential.

During my career, I participated in so many board meetings where we focused the conversation mostly on what, not who, or how. We did not focus Attention on people, which in any organisation is the source of all creative and conscious Action. Nobody ever wondered about the source of energy that powers the business activities and how it can be more abundant? This was always frustrating to me, particularly in creative businesses where the only thing they sell to their clients was their staff's ability to be present and access to creativity. Many businesses put in tools and management systems, make speeches and write reports, hoping that this is how businesses change and grow. Whilst some tools are useful in the short term, they will eventually be abandoned as they actually don't work that well and push against the very thing that made the business valuable and joyful.

Getting out of the way

What do I mean by connecting to waves of potential? Well, it's connecting to the source of all action, ideas, senses, thoughts and observations, as they arise instantaneously from a field of possibilities. In theoretical quantum sciences, it's known as the unified field. In yoga, Brahman. It's a space that modern meditation processes can help tap into and, with practice, inhabit. Let me explain.

When I paint, and in the past designed buildings and master planned towns and neighbourhoods, I use what I call Conscious Action. There are three aspects to this: **product, process and presence**. I can look at one of my completed paintings and say yes, it's an output, an object or *product* resulting from a particular creative process. I can also look at the *process* I'm undertaking to create the painting. I can also look at the empty sheet of paper and be *present* at the very moment my hand and paint take Action. The key aspect here is that, from the start, I tap into the source of all possibilities and then, with the right mindset, allow the potential to drive the entire process.

Getting out of the way of that flow is conscious Action. Modern meditation methods allow me to direct my Attention and dive deep into the moment the Action starts and then observe as the wave of potential continues to fuel the process. Fundamental to the success and joy of the whole thing is my ability to consciously observe the whole harmonious flow. There is no purpose to output other than to keep the flow going.

I don't interfere or waste energy and Attention on the final part because that lifts me out of the moment and stifles the flow with the expectation of any future outcome. This is all about what quality of perception, Attention and sense of *being* I can bring to my *doing* to any situation, any task, any event. The fact is, it's easy to explain this experience when doing something creative. The point is, *we can do any activity this way*. Practitioners of this will discover even the most everyday activity will turn itself into a creative action as you apply Attention to the source and process and not the imagined outcome or relationship to it.

Where does this stuff come from?

It might seem hard to see the world in this way, but it really isn't. Such shifts of perception, or should I say deepening Awareness, is a well-known aspect to yoga meditation. The three parts I described earlier are defined in yoga as the *known, knowing,* and *knower* referred to as the *Triputi* or the triad of a subject–object relationship.

The *known* refers to the object or the external world, including everything that can be perceived through the senses, such as people, objects, events, thoughts, feelings and ideas.

The *knowing* refers to the faculty of Awareness or consciousness that perceives the known. It is the inner ability to recognize, understand, and interpret the external world. This is often referred to as knowing *the field of doing.*

The *knower* refers to the individual Self. This is you as unbounded, absolute consciousness and is the source of all. It is regarded as the eternal and unchanging essence of the individual that observes and experiences the known and the knowing.

The goal, according to yoga philosophy, is the unity of the knower, the knowing, and the known. This is known as Samadhi, a state of complete absorption and oneness with the universe, where the individual Self merges with the universal consciousness.

A deeply creative act

Meditation practices are designed to know and access this oneness, which is located where Being and Doing intersect. It opens up what philosophers call the *intuition of the instant,* where a transformative and creative power can be discovered operating at the heart of the moment. Such a shift in insight requires a mind, body, senses, and the active material and spatial world, because creativity doesn't work on its own; it has to be in constant dialogue with the world through the senses. That's what being present means. When Being and Doing intersect, subject and object merge. This is what meditation is - a deep act of simultaneous reception and perception which is ultimately a creative act of observation and participation, so that the passive (being) and the active (doing) are inseparable. This is what an artist would call *inspiration*, an athlete being in the *zone*, a performer; *flow* and an engineer; *rightness*.

Pulled or pushed along?

We might not achieve full transcendence, but we all have moments where we feel one with the world and what we are doing in it. This is what meditation is for, and with practice, anyone and everyone can know this state anywhere, anytime.

Using modern meditation enables the practitioner to draw Attention to that space of flow. It connects us to a deeper sense of knowing, shaping how and what we do. With practice, we may feel pulled along or sometimes as I do pushed forward in the small of the back or from the centre of the chest. The body feels light and energised, action, whatever you are doing feels effortless and right and heart and mind full of possibilities. We create for ourselves a space where a sort of engineered or designed serendipity emerges as we act in the world. Every action we do seems to link purposefully to the next, the next, and the next.

Try it now.

We can apply this to both our working and personal lives. This is how we change the world.

It's a place you will recognise
because it's **home.**

One of my favourite artists, Albert Irvin [8], described his work as wanting to express that 'inextinguishable life force that carries us through' and express the 'elements of creation' with 'colour, gesture, shape, structure.' And that is pretty much what I hope to show you here.

You don't need to be an artist to know this. Artists are people who make a living intuitively knowing this. The question is, *what are your elements of creation?* What colours, gestures, shapes and structures through living your life consciously can you bring to the world – they will be different for everyone. All you need to do is find out how.

A Depiction and Eight Simple Shifts

We start with a simple 8 part depiction.

Throughout my career as an architect, I often drew simple diagrams to help illustrate core design principles or *tactics* that helped explain the *mechanics*, the how and why a particular design solution works. I do the same now in my Modern Meditation coaching and teaching. Figure 1 introduces the basic mechanics of the practice, from the insight that we all live life as a duality (inside and outside) to how different techniques unify this experience. You can see it's a simple process as each diagram builds step by step charting how the different techniques and practices work together. It all concludes with the Modern Meditation tracker to help with your day-to-day practice.

---

8. *Albert Irvin, Royal Academy. https://shop.royalacademy.org.uk/albert-irvin-obe-ra-untitled-opus-w-5-framed*

Figure 1. The mechanics of Modern Meditation practice

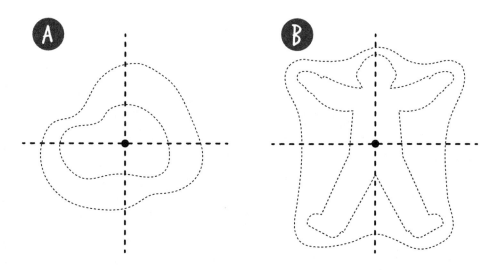

A. Starting Point: Within the depths of your being lies a captivating duality, an intricate blend of two realms – one characterised by consciousness and the other by changing matter. In the realm of yoga, this dual existence is referred to as "prakriti," the cause of your body, senses, and deeds – the very essence of nature at play. The second realm is known as "purusha," the architect of your vital essence, the force behind your animated existence.

B. Observing this duality, a convergence transpires, intertwining these two realms, manifesting as you on the planet, materialised as an unified harmonised field of potentiality.

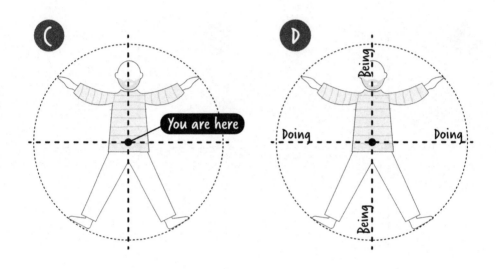

C. *We can intuitively know this fusion as an inner and outer reality, delineated here as the horizontal and vertical axes of experience, each bearing its own nature. You are located where these two dimensions cross.*

D. *We can name these axes, "being" and "doing". The intersection of these dimensions forms a node that defines existence, the locus where your engagement with the world unfolds from the inside out – where your unique essence finds expression.*

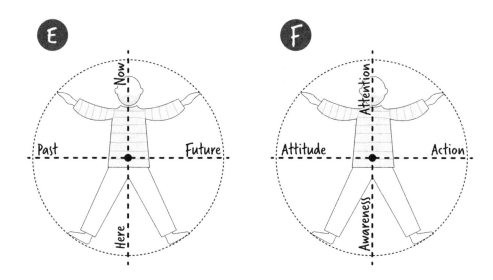

E. This node point can also be defined as the "eternal present," an immeasurable but knowable point in space in which you dwell. Here you are perpetually receptive to the countless prospects, opportunities and joy encompassing and flowing through you.

F. Modern meditation is then a contemporary exploration of this insight guided by the four 'A' skills. Through practice, it reshapes your centre, illuminating your perspective from within, radiating outward to transform your perception of the external world.

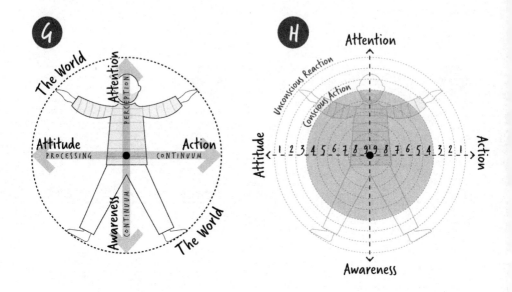

G. With practice, you'll traverse a path leading to an interconnected continuum of heightened consciousness and unleashed creative action, as soon as you understand how to process and perceive experience as a meditation.

H. To maintain your practice everyday, use the tracker as your guide, aiding you in accessing conscious, deliberate Action wherever you are in whatever you are doing.

The first diagram (A) depicts an undefined open space or shape through which two single lines, vertical and horizontal, cross at the centre. The outer field represents outer experience, Doing, and the inner cross or node point represents Being. The two axes depict the four core modern meditation skills which will eventually unify the outer and inner experience. As we progress through the process, the lines will represent different meditation skills as the meditation process grows.

The evolving diagrams and supporting texts in this book will support new shifts in how you perceive and process yourself and the world you inhabit. They will begin to equip you with new insights and tools to help change from the inside out. They are simple to follow and designed specifically for YOU, with all your worries, challenges and opportunities. Each is underpinned by a simple diagram consisting of two intersecting axes, horizontal and vertical, representing your inner and outer world joined at a singular node point. This node point is key. It represents where your inner and outer worlds connect in balance and coherence. All the techniques here are designed to help you know and use those lines. Modern Meditation will help you draw your insight along these lines inwards until you can hold yourself there at the node point. The node is you at your most fundamental, local to you as a specific individual, but simultaneously part of something universal.

To help you develop and deepen your practice, the nature and value of these axes will change. The first four steps are designed to help you refine and shift ideas and observations you may have collected over the years that may be defined in a limited way who you **think** you are. Treat these first four steps as preparing the ground for change and a basis for a new perspective. The next four steps will take you through the practice ending on the tracker, designed to help you make your everyday world a meditation.

As you follow the diagram, imagine yourself as a camera, gradually bringing the world into focus. Each of the eight shifts is an individual 'click' on the lens wheel as you turn experience into sharp relief. They are moments in the process of self-discovery, not levels or destinations. Treat the first four steps as something you are and the second four as something you do.

Shift One – Who Are You?
This shift begins with seeing yourself in a completely different way. You might look at yourself in the mirror every day but what you see is very limited. You are at your most fundamental, an unbounded flowing experience of inner and outer worlds.

Shift Two – Where Are You?
To know this duality, you will discover how to fix and locate this new sense of you. The you that is at the intersection between your inner and outer worlds your Being and Doing.

Shift Three – When Are You?
Then you will sharpen that sense of location by revealing that the intersection point is the **Here and Now,** the **eternal present** in the centre of everything.

Shift Four – What Are You?
This next step formalises how to change how you perceive and process the world differently. This next step introduces four key Modern Meditation skills, Conscious **Attention, Awareness, Attitude** and **Action** required to keep your perspective at the centre where everything you need to shape *what you are* can be found.

Shift Five – Strategies for developing Conscious Attention

This will be your first perception practice and perhaps the most important. You will see what attention is, how to switch it on from the inside out and direct and use it with purpose.

Shift Six – Strategies for developing Conscious Awareness

From attention developed and managed in the right way emerges the space within which Modern Meditation works, your deep inner awareness. This is you perceiving the world and yourself at a very different level.

Shift Seven – Strategies for developing Conscious Attitude

Then you shift into how you process what you perceive. Here your Modern Meditation skills will shift the world for you and light up your day-to-day reality.

Shift Eight – Strategies for developing Conscious Action

Then, finally, you learn how to make everything you do a meditation. The world will flow for you with meaning, purpose and intention, so you are free to Be and Do what you are.

The world will flow for you with meaning, purpose and intention, so you are free to Be and Do what you are.

Reflective Moment

Reflect here on how **happiness, creativity and joy are closely related to how you see and participate in the world**.

The World Three steps to happiness, creativity and joy	YOU Where and how can you do this?
Get involved in the action, the doing of the world. It's constant, happening through you and all around you. But take part selflessly. Work to help and support others always and never think about what's in it for you.	
Undertaking step I reveals your real nature and identity. You begin to see who and what you are, what you are good at and what you are for. You are here to learn and grow.	
Step II leads you to know that you are a vehicle, a conduit, an instrument through which love, creative potential, and joy flow into the world. So get out of the way – which brings us back to step I, where you work to keep the whole cycle going. The result is wellbeing and happiness for you and everyone else involved.	

Chapter 2

THE POSSIBILITIES ARE INFINITE

'If the doors of perception were cleansed then everything would appear to man as it is, Infinite. For man has closed himself up, till he sees all things through narrow chinks of his cavern.'

William Blake

Modern Meditation is designed to sharpen your perception of the world and maximise how you process the experience of it. Changes to how you perceive and process the world are fundamental skills and central to meditation practice. You will purposefully switch on to an inner state of full coherence that seems to come out from deep inside linked to what is happening outside. The world will feel full of possibilities. Many explorers in raising human consciousness and enhanced perception all report similar outcomes.

Of course, we have to have filters. If you got up one morning and saw everything as infinite and boundless, you might decide not to go to the office or get groceries. We have to work; we have to eat. When Blake writes 'infinite', read – potentiality. You are free and boundless.

Switching On

Practising Modern Meditation has one objective. To help you make the unconscious conscious. The practice will set you free and put you in charge because, as Jung said, 'Until you make the unconscious conscious, it will direct your life and you will call it fate.'

According to some neuroscientists, we are conscious of only about 5 per cent of our cognitive activity, so most of our decisions, perceptions, actions, emotions, and behaviour occur in 95 per cent of unconscious mind–body activity. From the beating of our hearts to pushing the shopping trolley around the store, you rely on something called the adaptive unconscious, which is the many ways that your mind and body understands and negotiates the world. The *adaptive unconscious* makes it possible for us to, say, walk down a busy street without having to go through complicated, strategic calculations to avoid colliding with other people or street signs.

The key is not to switch off this adaptive unconsciousness because that would be a disaster. We need this amazing ability to act in the world and filter what's important so that we can function without getting run over by a bus. But we will be learning to *watch and observe*, to shift your *Attention* to the flow of this constant *automatic* process, making the unconscious conscious.

Adaptive unconsciousness is your mind and body aligning with a deeper intelligence in **Action**. Often you might find yourself acting before any decision is made. This is an aspect of life which can be exciting but also, if we don't pay attention, gets us into trouble. But our main problem is that while the adaptive reaction occurs in the body, our minds can be elsewhere. What, where or who is that missing 5 per cent, and if we are not aware of 95 per cent of our actual experience, which is actually happening to us, where are we?

If you think about it, this means if an average life expectancy is 85 years, we are only fully awake and conscious for about four years and three months. It's likely, too, that most of that time was before adulthood. What a waste. Perhaps this is why so many people close to the end sadly say, *where has my life gone?* Something or someone has to be the actual experiencer of the whole 100 per cent; otherwise, what's it all for?

No Names Please

You, everybody and everything else is, at their most fundamental, fields of flowing potential energy. What shapes and utilises this energy into something useful, with intention, is *information*. Combined, energy and information form the deep ground of intelligence, an ultimate consciousness manifesting and fuelling everything we experience, including our experience of experiencing.

This notion of you as pure consciousness is not new. But it has nothing to do with concepts, names, identities, wants, or any other view you might have about yourself and others. That needs to change because they are illusions. You are born, you die, and all the stuff in between is theory, and if you let them, mostly, somebody else's. If you have often suspected that your self-image, isn't you, you are on a path of transformation.

In-formation

Everything is information. Or as I like to say *in-formation*. Your innate ability for consciousness and to undertake Conscious Action in the world is a matter of how you **perceive** and **process** this in-formation. Everything manifested inside your field of experience right now, received by your senses, is being assembled, expressed, connected and dis-connected. It's a continuous process. There is no real division between you and the things you experience. Your thoughts, feelings, emotions, body, brain, nervous system and actions are all interconnected. They intermingle, shape each other and appear tangible, solid and real, thus creating the world around you.

> There is no real division between you and the things you experience.

And it's all flowing beautifully inside a continuous field of **NOW**. Until that is, we, as people, interfere with it all. Every experience you and I have is in the NOW. Moment by moment, your mind, combined with your body, is a transceiver of the NOW. They receive and transmit in-formation. But the quality of this in-formation, its effectiveness and authenticity, and how you utilise it are shaped by how *you* perceive and process it. And this is exactly what I mean by **being conscious.** It involves a particular type of paying Attention.

However, being conscious doesn't mean thinking about stuff and then more thinking about stuff. In fact, it doesn't involve thinking at all. There is more to it, and it's here we dip tentatively into yoga science and theoretical physics to define what consciousness is.

Scientists, particularly quantum physicists like David Bohm [9] (with his work with Jiddu Krishnamurti), concluded that the human body, mind or even the universe are ultimately not material, composed of molecules or atoms, subject to external mechanical forces. Instead, everything is seen as one endless energy field. We are the fabric of the universe, composed of particles, waves or strings of information, a limitless field, forever in flux and transformation. In Bohm's own words:

'Space is not empty. It is full, a plenum as opposed to a vacuum, and is the ground for the existence of everything, including ourselves. The universe is not separate from this cosmic sea of energy.'

Unified Field

Your experience of consciousness depends then on how you perceive, process and experience this field. Modern Meditation takes these concepts and simplifies them into fields of Being and Doing, which themselves (if you choose to notice) are constantly interlinked as one unified field of *aliveness*. Modern Meditation practice will take you beyond physical structures, form and matter into the deep space of absolute consciousness from which they emerge.

---

9. Moody, D.E. 'An Uncommon Collaboration. David Bohm and J. Krishnamurti'. Krishnamurti Foundation America. https://www.kfa.org/krishnamurti-bohm-program/

As Bohm concluded, everything flows in a state of undivided wholeness [10] in which all parts of the universe, including the observer [you and me] and his/her/their instruments [mind and body], merge into one totality.

This suggests that the world, as we experience it, is fundamentally tied up with our ability to be knowingly conscious, which probably explains why the planet is in crisis now.

So while you may feel disconnected and separate, labelled, judged, mentally stressed and isolated, lost and subject to forces beyond your control, that is an illusion and can be changed.

'And in that state of communion—if you inquire more deeply—you will find that you are not only in communion with nature, with the world, with everything about you, but also in communion with yourself.'

Krishnamurti

---

10. Storoy, D. 'David Bohm, Implicate Order and Holomovement'. Science & Non-Duality.com. https://www.scienceandnonduality.com/article/david-bohm-implicate-order-and-holomovement

Reflective Moment

Use this space to write, draw or just sit.

You are free and boundless.

Can you recall a moment when you have felt at the peak of your powers and that anything was possible? Do you remember a joyful experience, free and spontaneous but at the same time insightful and purposeful? Did it feel effortless beyond description, names and reward?

Chapter 3

CREATIVE ACTION

'Through our eyes, the universe is perceiving itself. Through our ears, the universe is listening to its harmonies. We are the witnesses through which the universe becomes conscious of its glory, of its magnificence.' [11]

Alan Watts

Much of my career has been centred on perception and how to perceive differently. In a sense, this book is all about perception. Everything in the world depends on perception, your ability to *see* and then *know*. But, these days, education does very little to help students develop their **knowing** abilities or non-verbal skills. We need to teach consciousness-based techniques to nurture intuition, spontaneity, playfulness, connectivity and creative action. Only these essential human skills will save us, as they are vital to a purposeful, meaningful life.

---

11. Alan Watts, quoted in *The Best Alan Watts Quotes*, David Crombie and Catriona Jardine, Crombie Jardine, 2016.

And as David Bohm says:

'Such insight implies an original and creative act of perception into all aspects of life, mental and physical, both through the senses and through the mind, and this is perhaps the true meaning of meditation.' [12]

There is nothing new in this. About 3000 BCE, ancient yoga texts described this field of consciousness as a universal ground of absolute reality from which everything emerges. When yogis talk about the Self (*Atma*), it's defined as our core but simultaneously contained in a deeper ground of reality. This idea of inner–Self is not to be confused with the more *surface* aspects of your mind, body and ego. They are separate. Determining and distinguishing between the two is a key skill and the start of becoming whole again. With meditation practice, you get to know and feel this in three ways. Yogis have a term for it: – **'sat chit ananda'** – *existence, consciousness, joy.* *Sat* is existence, *chit* is consciousness and *ananda* is joy.

In other words, if you are alive, there is consciousness, and if there is consciousness, there is joy. Many problems stem from our propensity to ignore this trinity or treat them as discrete entities. In reality, they are one and found in each other. When all three are in full coherence, it's considered the highest plane of existence. They are not a target, though. The benefits

12. Storoy, D. 'David Bohm, Implicate Order and Holomovement'. Science & Non-Duality.com.
https://www.scienceandnonduality.com/article/david-bohm-implicate-order-and-holomovement

come from working your way towards this state. Intention and practice are key. It's all in the process, and you only need to do two things.

1. Change the way you perceive in-formation.

2. Change the way you process in-formation.

This is the core of my Modern Meditation practice. Luckily, you already have these capacities, and with meditation, you turn them into life-transforming skills.

Are You Created or Creative?

When you learn to meditate and **see** the world and yourself more clearly, you begin to wake up to a life-changing realisation which reveals that some of us are **created** by the world while others **create** it. The difference between the two is simply that old yoga maxim – *'to be in the world and not of it'*. People who are created don't generally see very much. People who are creators see everything.

> People who are creators
> see everything.

Those that are *created* live in a constant state of *distraction* and *attachment*. It's easy to be created these days. We are constantly bombarded with concepts and images regarding how we should be in the world. We are labelled, named, numbered and divided as we become more and more manipulated by continuous algorithms that follow and feed off our every emotionally fuelled Action. Our Attention has become monetised as somebody else's business model, as our ability to know what is real, what is actually needed, becomes blurred. We now fret about how we look, what others think, and what tribe we belong to, resulting in agitation and fear, which diminishes us all as we try to affirm reality to ourselves and others. We might do this by following and sharing trends on social media or posting updates to show our postcard life of wonderful days out, holidays or even updates on our wellbeing or lack of it. Nothing is wrong with this, except it perpetuates the illusion that this version of the world is *all* there is. Yoga science tells us that agitation is due to a delusional state called *maya* – literally translated as a 'cloud of appearance'. In the end, that's all Instagram, TikTok and Facebook often are.

Conscious Endeavour

Stop for a moment and think about where you might be right now – are you being **created** by others, or are you **creating** for yourself?

If you create your world, you see yourself and your environment differently. You are **awake**, utilising your innate ability for **conscious endeavour** – to be consciously active inside the flow of in-formation rather than just unconsciously reactive. As Henry Thoreau tells us about the 'highest of arts' in *Walden*:

'It is something to be able to paint a particular picture, carve the statue, and so make an object beautiful; but it is far more glorious to carve and paint the very atmosphere and medium through which we look, which morally we can do to affect the quality of the day, that is the highest of arts.'

Are you affecting the 'quality of the day', and if so, how? Are you paying full attention to the smallest in-formation as if it was the most important thing? Are you awake to who you really are, what you are doing or are you just going through the motions on autopilot, not paying attention to the information for you?

The 'highest of the arts' is to know that you and the universe are the same. There is no out there. There is no me or you. There is just one continuous **NOW** through which everything is manifest. When you get this, when you 'see' it, not only can you influence your reality, but you can also actually create it. All you need to do is turn your **attention inwards** towards NOW because it's located right where you are. This is the key to Modern Meditation. It's not a question of faith or belief but direct experience. That's what meditation is for. You and I create the world we see, inhabit and operate in. This is insight, or 'inner – sight'.

Going Inwards

First, it is learning to not only **Do** but **Be** as well. Too many of us are locked into a type of perpetual doing – a never-ending whirlpool of expectations, goals, wants, desires, status, aversions and demands etc... how many of those so-called *needs* are real, healthy or helpful. And how many of those *must-do* impulses have been *artfully* (I'm talking about advertising and social media or even your employer here) instilled into how you perceive and process the world?

So ask yourself – do you feel overwhelmed, tired, anxious, angry, frustrated and disappointed, or empowered, purposeful, motivated and full of energy? Being created by the world, *being of the world*, means you are caught up in events with little control as you fall through a life that goes mostly unnoticed and unlived, shaped by one unconscious reaction after the other.

Creating means *being in the world*. To wake up to a constant, empowering, flowing process of Conscious Action and endeavour. As Thoreau hints, it involves shifting your perception and learning to touch and be enlivened by the part of you that is the source of YOU and your world every moment of your life – your **True Self.** The experience of this is flowing, moment-to-moment conscious awareness of the infinite potential that will only manifest once you learn to turn your attention towards it, observe it and let it flow through you and be you.

So where do you go to **know** this? You go inwards. You have to understand what the Self is and, perhaps more importantly, what it isn't.

First, you can't access this **knowing** via finely tuned intellectual faculties. This deeper sense of knowing comes through cultivating distinctive mindsets and outlooks that, taken together, give rise to more powerful intuition.

It's a Quantum Thing

You tap into something that's always been there, but nobody has likely bothered to show you until now. And it will be a rediscovered profound blossoming that will flow through your mind–body, pervading every cell and neuron you have. It will change the way you interact, experience and perceive the world around you, which in turn transforms the world for you. Practising Modern Meditation is a quantum thing – *change how you observe the world, and the world changes.*

There are five common aspects of this changed experience, providing momentum and direction to new insight. These are interconnected aspects of knowing and tapping into your Self through Modern Meditation.

1. **Space** – Is everything, and it's not as empty as you may assume. You will notice space opens between you and the world, you and your thoughts and feelings. That space is actually full and contains your potential for change. Recognise this space as a connector and not a barrier.

2. **Time** – Becomes an illusion. Clock time is psychological, so as you change what you think is time passing, it bends and expands. Deadlines will never be stressful again.

3. **Need** – You will notice that all the stuff you thought you needed to be useful and successful in the world shifts too. You are already complete and pretty much self–sufficient.

4. **Connection** – Any feeling of isolation and separation will fall away. Not only do you feel more connected to others, but

you'll also feel connected to something bigger. You'll never feel lost or unsure about what to do.

5. **Wholeness** – Finally, you will see that the world isn't made up of individuals fragmented into different groups, tribes, religions, politics, etc. – none of that is ultimately real. You, me, the world, and the universe are whole.

So far, so good, but you might think, how is that done? – I am so busy, so tangled up with what I need to do every day, so stressed and overwhelmed trying to keep everything going that if I change now, it will all collapse around me!

Well, that's the whole point. I am not asking you to stop what you are doing. Instead, I invite you to do it differently. Rather than let the world overwhelm you with endless external demands of must and should (mostly in your head anyway), you tackle everything from the inside out – from the very source of You. If we are to save ourselves and the world, this simple shift needs to underpin all 21st-century endeavours.

Figure 2: A new model for 21st century life and work placing who you are at the core of what you do.

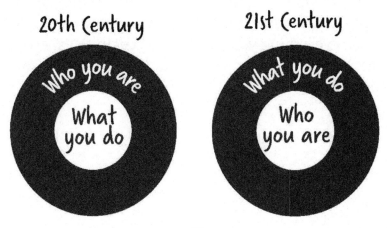

Making Change Your Intention

To start, I invite you to explore the power of Modern Meditation with a deep feeling and certainty with your entire body and mind. Meditation is a whole body-mind thing, so make it your intention to explore yourself.

I mentioned earlier that you are a field of potential. You are the change you seek. You are the change that has to happen; that *is* happening. To allow this potential to flow, focus on and develop your intention. It must feel like it's in the present tense – i.e.: *'I am changing'* – not *'I want to change.'*. This is important because acknowledging your inner potential is fundamental to presence. An intention that suggests – *sometime in the future, I will be happy* – is pointless. Your intention has to be shaped in the present tense because it's impossible to **become** happy; you can only **be** happy.

Your intention will be like a felt, inner agreement with yourself. You will know when a particular mindset, speech, action or response works against your intention as you feel a momentary shift in balance and energy. This isn't a disaster; treat them as little messages emerging from the inside that will help you get back on track. After a while, you will know how to affirm your intention in everything you do. You will begin to experience a deeper nature and sense of self – your True Self. This shift will serve you to go further.

Reflective Moment

Use this space to write, draw or just sit.

Are you created or creative?

When you learn to meditate and **see** the world and yourself more clearly, you begin to wake up to a life-changing realisation which reveals that some of us are **created** by the world while others **create** it. Jot down 10 aspects where you feel and see where your life is in and out of your control. Be honest and uncritical. Just process your perception as it is.

Created?	Creative?

Chapter 4

RESPONDING TO YOUR OWN NATURE

'To transform the world, we must begin with ourselves; and what is important in beginning with ourselves is the **intention**.'

Jiddu Krishnamurti

To start *creating,* you need to work with where you are and what you have. You can't start from zero. You have to have something to work from. In Modern Meditation, you start with – your own *nature*. This is the ground on which you start to build. Importantly, you are not in the business of removing or demolishing your nature but progressively changing your relationship with it. Using Modern Meditation based practises, you can create new ways your nature operates.

This is your first insight, and it's in three parts:

1. You begin to focus on your body and understand that it is an amazing, adaptable instrument for your conscious True Self to act through.

2. Then you turn your attention to your thinking, seeing that your mental habits, feelings, emotions and assumptions are just that – habits you have accumulated and are also part of the instrument and not the True Self

3. Then you understand that the mass of information, ideas and opinions that you constantly pick over, stored in your unconscious mind, will, if allowed, shape and override what is really happening, who you really are, and what you can do.

Everybody's *behaviour* is rooted in a cycle of thoughts, habits and actions. It's a mistake to think of your nature as the real YOU and to think that it's so defining and fixed that it's impossible to change. If that were the case, how would you or anybody change and grow? The solution is to develop an internal process where you can progressively improve, open and transform it towards a more purposeful, accurate version of yourself in the world.

Unconscious Reaction

Let's examine this process of nature more closely. We might now call it your unconscious reactivity to the world around you.

At one level, the world is given to you as it is. But on another, you also simultaneously create it. For each of us, the world fundamentally depends upon how we see, think and feel about it. You obviously don't bring the world into existence, but you do a great deal in transforming and shaping it into what you assume is an actual, coherent and stable thing that supports and allows you to do what you want. In other words, we project our own version of the world over the top of what is already inherently there.

It all starts with your senses and nervous system. Your neural network is a transceiver. It receives information about the world and responds by transmitting you in the shape of your actions and thoughts back out again. Your problem lies in how you perceive and process this in-formation flow. Most of us tend to interfere with the flow according to our assumptions and prejudices. This, in turn, changes how reality is for us and how we respond.

'A great many people think they are thinking when they are merely rearranging their prejudices.'

David Bohm

This interference is a deeply embedded, largely unconscious system of likes and dislikes, which propels your thoughts, desires, wants, and actions. Over time, they become deeply imprinted into your mind and body. And it's a continuous process, a closed loop that is ever-changing and adapting according to what you think you want or see.

Your ego is principally running the show and interfering with the whole process. But that doesn't mean change isn't possible. In fact, learning to become aware and seeing the system in operation by shifting how you *perceive* it is the start of your transformation.

Running the Programme

You may never have been aware of this process because it's a habitual, adaptive unconscious process. Your mind/body is the interface between you and the world. It comes with an inbuilt intelligence that helps it process and operate without you as the so-called *conscious operator* getting involved. This is your nature, or better still, nature in you running according to its programme.

So let's examine its parts. You can see five elements overlapping and interconnecting.

Figure 3. How the narrative of unconscious reactivity works.

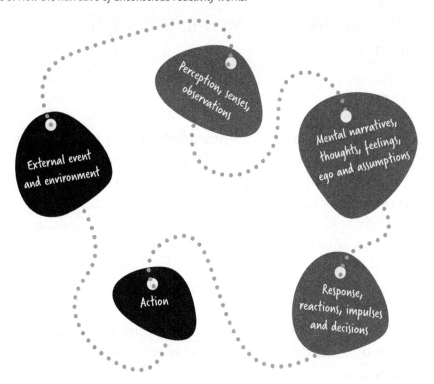

There is no real beginning or end. You can start anywhere on the loop. Let's say a particular event happens at work. This is your external environment/event. The first thing that happens is that you perceive it. This is you receiving raw in-formation before making any judgement. Once the in-formation is received instantly, your ego kicks in and activates a particular sequence of thoughts and feelings. This fuels an internal mental narrative, your *inner critic*, which prompts a certain reaction or impulse. This energy needs to be expressed as action, which takes many forms, from something internal and emotional to an external action. The action feeds into the external world, only to fuel the whole process again.

This process, of course, happens at great speed and goes mostly unnoticed. Our egos clog up the system, so we can't *see* clearly and *respond* accurately. And remember, even though most of this is happening inside our heads, we are barely conscious of it at least 95 per cent of the time. We think about what's happening, not what is happening, as we act according to our *'nature'*.

You might notice when you look this way that there is a space to live life differently once you develop perspective. It's likely the real insight here is how many of your thoughts and feelings and following actions were unnecessary. Doing so gives truth to the insight that if you want to change reality, you have to change how you perceive and process it from the inside out. When you unconsciously react, you simply function via a set of learned, habitual tendencies. You are going through the motions because your body knows how to act, to move. So when you are reacting in this way, you are not really taking part in what is really happening, only in what you think is happening. Worse still, your attention is connected to a stream of thinking, either trying to reconcile a half-remembered past or shape an imagined future. In other words, you are not present, which takes a lot of energy. It can be exhausting.

Unfortunately, this is all too common in our human condition. This state is called the brain's 'Default Mode Network (DMN)'.

Research [13] reveals that the DMN regularly grabs our attention, stimulating our brain to wander aimlessly in problematic, recursive, self-referential, negative thinking and emotions. For many, this is what normal everyday life is. This explains why obsessively thinking and feeling this way makes us feel dissatisfied, isolated and unhappy. The DMN can hold us hostage in mental worlds, which overwhelm our ability to engage and be fully conscious of things as they are. As we wrestle with the world this way, the loop tightens, and we feel there is no way out.

Learning to *observe* in meditation, you'll soon realise that these narratives *think* themselves. There is no thinker. They don't have any explicit goal other than to satisfy learned or received prejudices about the world, others and yourself – and none of it is real. It's no surprise that research detects links between overactivity in the DMN and mental distress like stress, anxiety and depression.

> Learning to observe in meditation, you'll soon realise that these narratives think themselves. There is no thinker.

What Does Science Say?

Many assume meditation puts the brain into deep relaxation or even switches it off. It's not the case because the brain begins to operate at a higher, much healthier and more powerful level.

---

13. Brewer, J.A., et al. 'Meditation experience is associated with differences in default mode network activity and connectivity', Proc Natl Acad Sci U S A, 13 Dec 2011;108(50):20254-9. doi: 10.1073/pnas.1112029108. Epub 2011 Nov 23. PMID: 22114193; PMCID: PMC3250176

Meditation isn't about switching off your DMN because you need it. We only have a terrible habit of filling up our DMN with useless stuff, which is mostly negative. And because the DMN is where your ego and flight-fight response reside, you may, unwittingly, be fuelling its overactive and distorted operation. It's known that meditation practice can disrupt and reduce the negative impact of the DMN cycle via open, non-attached observation cultivated in Modern Meditation practice. Principally, by *unconditionally observing* using Modern Meditation techniques, you will shift something mostly unconscious into something conscious. Instead of being whirled about by your overstimulated, rapidly revolving DMN, you see that it's not actually you at all. This is the start of working towards better wellbeing from the inside out. [14]

Getting Stuck

In yoga science, these habitual, deep-thinking patterns are called *Samskaras*. These are described as mental grooves, cut by thoughts as they travel through the mind. They are hard to get out of. This is why if you are constantly taxed about something or suffering from a negative series of thoughts, it feels hard to escape. Repeated actions and thoughts will create more grooves in your mind, which for some becomes addictive. An everyday example of this entrapment can be seen almost everywhere. How many people do you notice wandering around looking at a smartphone? It's like they are being led along the street by whatever they are watching on the screen. They are barely

14. Garrison K.A., et al. 'Meditation leads to reduced default mode network activity beyond an active task', Cogn Affect Behav Neurosci, Sep 2015;15(3):712-20. doi: 10.3758/s13415-015-0358-3. PMID: 25904238; PMCID: PMC4529365.

conscious of where they are or what they are doing, yet they seem to have not even noticed.

Being caught up in a groove of thinking like this is why people will say, 'I just can't stop thinking about it' or 'I just can't see a way out'. We've all been there wandering aimlessly along the bottom of each Samskara valley, often with rising anxiety and never seeing a way out.

The idea is to shift your perspective towards a better viewpoint. So, not only can you see where the valley is leading, but also a wider landscape beyond, offering the opportunity to break free. To do this requires a shift from unconscious reaction to Conscious Action. Modern Meditation is Conscious Action.

Reflective Moment

Use this space to write, draw or just sit.

With this little exercise, you can try and make each part of the cycle conscious. Consider an event you experienced, maybe with a friend, family member or work colleague. Now, using the chart, try and break it down into distinct parts in terms of what happened and what might have happened if you were to see it all happening from a distance.

Study your answers and then ask yourself:

- Am I ultimately defined by the contents of my unconscious mode?

- Is that what propels and shapes me, or is there something missing?

- Can I use it and then change it?

Moment	What I did	What I wish I did
1. External Event		
2. Perception		
3. Mental Response		
4. Reaction Impulse		
5. Action		

Chapter 5

CONSCIOUS ACTION

'He who knows in truth this spirit and knows nature with its changing conditions, wherever this man/woman may be, they are no more whirled around by fate.'

The Bhavagad Gita

So you might ask: Where is the opportunity for change? If I am just a cog in the whole process and hostage to my 'nature' via how I perceive, think, feel and act, what can I do to upgrade my nature? How do I become free from this cycle? Why should I try to manage my fate, take charge and act consciously?

The answer isn't to restrain or try to stop. Instead, the solution is to change your relationship to the whole thing. This is what I mean by a change of perspective. To find a place where you can simply observe the process underway without getting caught up. You can cultivate a different way of paying **Attention** and a different **Awareness** of what is happening, which will change your **Attitude** toward the **Action** you are invited to undertake.

Using the four Modern Meditation skills described in Chapter 1, you can reorientate into the centre of the whole process. You can go inwards and find a still point, a place of quiet observation. A safe lookout. You allow the world's whirl as you mentally experience it to flow around you. You are fully involved but operating in the whole process, not from attachment which will continue to place you at the edge of the loop where you're subjected to continuous buffering forces, but from its centre where it's still, expansive, calm and purposeful.

Again we can return to those artists that have helped define this experience. As the poet T.S. Eliot wrote, we exist at the:

'... still point of the turning world. Neither flesh nor fleshless; Neither from nor towards; at the still point, there the dance is, But neither arrest nor movement. And do not call it fixity, Where past and future are gathered.'

It might not be obvious at first, but this shift inwards to the centre puts you right into the heart of the action and source of your life.

Figure 4. Finding the still point

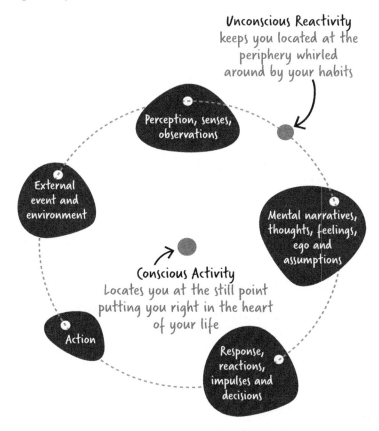

Unconscious Reactivity
keeps you located at the
periphery whirled
around by your habits

Perception, senses,
observations

External
event and
environment

Mental narratives,
thoughts, feelings,
ego and
assumptions

Conscious Activity
Locates you at the still point
putting you right in the heart
of your life

Action

Response,
reactions,
impulses and
decisions

This shift inwards to the centre puts
you right into the heart of the action and
source of your life.

This is the first and perhaps most important aspect of the four
Modern Meditation practices – **Attention**. The practice is paying
Attention to paying Attention.

This shift of perception into the centre will immediately upgrade
your world. You come in behind your senses, thoughts and
actions and process the in-formation received differently. A new

perception will unfold, capable of seeing the truth of you and the world, of things as they are. Going inwards and observing from there opens a powerful space of insight and awareness.

It's a place where you discover that it's not you operating *your* eyes that see, your hands that grasp, your ears that hear, your body that moves your mind that thinks. They act subject to your *nature*. They are simply the mind-body receiving in-formation. The real YOU is the observer, the authentic experience of what is really happening.

In Jack Hawley's translation of *The Bhagavad Gita*, [15] he tells us:

'All actions pertaining to bodily existence take place in the worldly self, which isn't the real Self... which is beyond all worldly matters.'

This quote is my constant companion. I read it again and again. Memorise it if you can. This amazing 5000-year-old realisation of the true nature of being human is what underpins our 21st-century Modern Meditation explorations.

15. Hawley, J. *The Bhagavad Gita. A Walkthrough for Westerners (New World Library, 2011)*

How Will It Feel?

Attention might start with how you undertake a task, handle and feel an object, or see the sky or trees in your street. It might start with how you move, walk, sit and stand. Feeling effortless and light, or how you respond or feel about someone, how you listen or what you say. How you work will change, and sometimes what you do will change too. It might start with an idea or an insight. Something you do. This is the difference between *unconscious reaction* and *conscious action*. You will feel the difference. It will feel like you are connected to something meaningful and powerful, and if you want it to, it can shape your world indefinitely wherever you are doing whatever you're doing.

Doing Your Thing

I want to finish with this important point I often make to my students. Discovering how to shift and find a place to *observe* and be conscious of the whole thing in Action has nothing to do with switching off or just going through the world in a detached, isolated way. This shift has nothing to do with stepping back, deciding not to have an opinion about the world or not getting fully involved. I'm afraid it's the opposite. You will suddenly wake up and understand you can and have to *affect the quality of the day* and, in doing so, the whole world.

You have responsibilities, and the more you practise Modern Meditation, the more you will get to know and act on them. This is what yoga wisdom calls knowing your *dharma* – living and working by your inner truth – your purpose in the world. The word *dharma* means – your position, where you stand. You will know what this means when you use these practices regularly, with intention and openness, without expectation. When you activate with Modern Meditation, you wake up to this inner truth. You transform. You take Action. I see this happening all the time when people follow my courses.

This last part is particularly important. It's easy to become distracted and convinced that the world needs to be challenged, shaped and wrestled with. That's how it feels to see everything and everybody as opposing forces, fragmented and divided. You develop a self-world view from your own subconscious reactions.

The Right Tools from the Right Place

Modern Meditation is observing with a particular emphasis on its application, not only as you sit in formal practice but as you move through the world doing what you do. Everything you do can become a meditation.

These are the right tools coming from the right place. You can apply them right in the centre of your daily operation – after all, that's exactly where you need to make an impact. This makes it ideally suited for the modern 21st-century world with all its complexities, complications, opportunities and stresses.

Some of my students report that **beanddo** techniques suddenly open up meditation practice for them:

'My relationship with meditation was frustrating and uncomfortable. I was beginning to understand there was more to yoga than asana and became interested in philosophy when I attended a beanddo day course and met Mick. That was the day meditation shifted for me. During the practises, I could feel something happening in my body that I'd never felt before, a vibrating energy I had never connected to consciously. I was fascinated and curious and found observing that energy is so much more powerful than simply following my breath.
The connection into consciousness and energy through the body was the ultimate game changer for me. Finding that point of a connection made everything else click into place. Mick's 'stay there' has become a familiar mantra in my practice to hold onto that connection in the initial calming down and letting go moments.'

Amelia,
beanddo trained Modern Meditation teacher

Finding that place, that point of observation, and with practice *staying there* is a game-changer.

Reflective Moment

Use this space to write, draw or just sit.

How you get in your own way

As I mentioned earlier, it's easy to assume that success in the world and what you do in it needs to be tested, judged, shaped, and wrestled with. That's how most organisations work from the outside-in. Reflect on the chart below and plot which side of the line you are mostly on.

How much do I get in my own way?			
Unconscious Reaction		**Conscious Reaction**	
Critical judgement and fear of action		Observe with no judgemental awareness as action happens	
Forcing a particular way of action		Trust that you have the tools and insight to make it work	
Trying hard to do it right		Let go and let it happen	
Determined focus on final product and output		Open focus on the process and experience until it flows	

PART TWO
CORE PRINCIPLES OF MODERN MEDITATION

'You do not need to leave your room. Remain sitting at your table and listen. Do not even listen, simply wait, be quiet, still and solitary. The world will freely offer itself to you to be unmasked, it has no choice, it will roll in ecstasy at your feet.'

~ *Franz Kafka*

Chapter 6

WHO ARE YOU?

'What's wrong with most people is that they have this block – they feel they could never make a difference, and therefore, they never face the possibility, because it is too disturbing, too frightening.'

David Bohm

The first thing is to see yourself as a duality. Forget all notions of identity, status and personality. Let's get straight to the primary, regulating, underlying principle of meditation: **You have an inside and an outside.**

Don't worry if this feels like a tricky yogic theory thing. It will come as you upgrade your senses and recalibrate your Attention as part of your Modern Meditation practice. The thing to know is that everything in the natural and human-made world has a centre and a periphery. Nothing can exist without this relationship. They rely on each other. It's the centre, the core, the source or purpose that gives rise to meaning, action and identity. For example, your town likely has a central square where the most important civic buildings and ceremonial events happen. It will be where people gravitate for celebration or demonstration. It might also be the centre of commerce too, perhaps a marketplace. In all creative works, we unknowingly follow this structure as all ideas are found in nature. Seeds, too, have a core embryo from which the plant grows. Our Solar System has a centre of energy, the Sun, while the Milky Way, like all galaxies, has at its centre a supermassive black hole around which Earth orbits every 225 million years.

This duality of inside/outside/here/there/ is our starting point. You, too, have an inside and outside which must work together if you want to operate in the world. This is your first shift of perspective. Not seeing yourself as a solid but as an open space, a field through which all experience flows.

To help, here is the first diagram. It's deceptively simple.

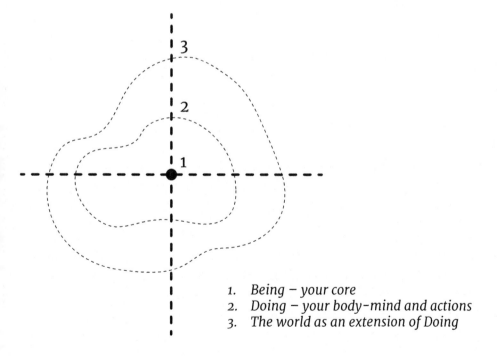

1. *Being – your core*
2. *Doing – your body-mind and actions*
3. *The world as an extension of Doing*

Figure 5: What are you? A duality as a mix of two interconnected fields of experience

Closely study this illustration, as it will change and develop as you progress.

Imagine you have been cut horizontally, revealing a cross-section through your life experience right now. Instead of seeing organs, muscle and skeletal structure, go deeper and see *fields of space* in which everything happens. You don't *see* this reality other than when these fields combine to manifest the person (the **you**) others see. But no doubt you can feel them.

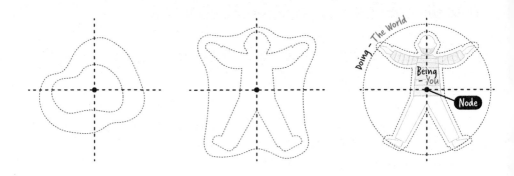

Figure 6: How the two fields of experience appear as you in the world.

At your core is a field of **Being** – that is, who you are at your most fundamental – *the Self*, as pure conscious awareness. You can't see this field, it's not precisely defined, but you know it's there because you can feel it; you are aware of it, as its whole reason for **Being** is to be known and expressed through you into the world. This field is responsible for your feeling of *aliveness*.

Outside as a flowing outer, the seemingly physical wrapper is your **Doing** field of action. That's you as a form, the mind/body as an instrument your BEING employs to be expressed as mind-body–action in the world. These two aspects are constantly flowing, interacting fields. Still, we are not usually aware of this aspect until we consciously experience and explore this duality and connection through Modern Meditation.

The very outer field – the world, is an extension of your Doing field, as the world has a continuous temporal flowing flux of events, action and experience. We might call this nature, of which your mind/body is part. Inside the field is your ego sense of I (me), your unconscious reaction, your Conscious Action, senses, thinking, birth, death, suffering and joy. Basically, it's the field through which your life plays out.

Unity

You might feel lost and perhaps not get this duality thing. If not, can you recall a time when you were doing something, and suddenly it all felt as if you were totally absorbed in the task? You didn't need to think or analyse as you seemed to know what to do as it flowed together. And with that sudden experience came a little joy and happiness. Well, you have, without intention, accidentally experienced non-dual wholeness. This is you aligning with the expectation of what life wants from you and not the other way around.

Describing and defining this double nature is useful, as it points to something you intuitively know – you are wired to know it. In meditation, you can perceive this duality and distinguish the inner from the outer constantly. Ironically, perceiving the duality removes duality, creating oneness and, thus, a deeper life experience. This double nature is often referred to in wisdom traditions as our 'dual condition', which for thousands of years, humanity has been trying to overcome. That's why meditation, when practised properly, is often referred to as a 'non-dual' or 'unitive' practice in that it will unify the duality and lead to innate moments of 'oneness' and 'wholeness'. In other words, you reach a state where all your ideas, decisions and actions are based on seeing the world clearly, shaped and defined by the inner realm of Conscious Awareness of Being.

> You reach a state where all your ideas, decisions and actions are based on seeing the world clearly, shaped and defined by the inner realm of Conscious Awareness of Being.

The important thing here is not to get caught up in assuming your inside/outside aspect has to do with the distinction between mind and body. It isn't. That's why at **beanddo**, we distinguish between **Being** and **Doing**. It might help here to delve deeper into the characteristics of each field.

Making a Line of Connection

Look at figure 5 again. You can see I have drawn an intersecting horizontal and vertical line which 'link fields together'. These lines represent the direction your Modern Meditation practice will take you. The key is to find your way onto these lines, stay on them, and let them guide you using the techniques described later. After a while, you'll easily follow these lines wherever you are, whatever you are doing. Meditation means following their 'natural' trajectory, linking your inner and outer worlds until you reach an 'easy and effortless' point of balance and equilibrium.

Where the horizontal and vertical lines intersect is who you are most fundamentally. This is you as pure Awareness – your Self! Some of my students report feeling this *anchoring* in their abdomen, belly, centre of the chest, around the heart or even between the eyebrows. Some say it feels like their whole body is infused. It doesn't matter where you feel this, as you know it as an internal experience linked to your mind–body and the world around you.

> Where the horizontal and vertical lines intersect is who you are at your most fundamental. This is you as pure Awareness – your Self!

Like a Mirror

Your next question might be, how do I know the difference between **Doing** and **Being**, and where is this sense of Self? The answer is to feel it all as different experiences through their relationship. It's through observing yourself unconditionally concerning people, things, places, events, thoughts and actions– the world around you right now. Modern Meditation techniques will enable you to become a highly polished 'mirror' reflecting your true Self accurately.

For example, an aspect can't be permanent unless we compare it to something impermanent. Something can't be observed unless there is an observer, and so on. This last one is key to Modern Meditation practice. It is a unifying link between them so that the observer and the observed become whole. That's where you come in as a *conscious, observing collaborator.*

Take a moment and reflect on this. It's not an intellectual exercise but more an intuitive feeling. If we assume we are nothing but the unconscious mental chatter and habitual reactive patterns of our mind–body, we miss the bigger picture. If, for example, you assume you are an individual determined by thoughts alone, then when we learn to *observe* our thinking from a distance, who or what is doing the observing here? To find a position to *watch* thoughts and feelings, and ultimately the actions as they arise, is when you know you are making progress in your meditation practice.

You can see that distinguishing between inside and outside brings a spatial dimension to this insight. This is a key starting point to feeling your way into Modern Meditation because, after a while, you notice a *space* between you and the world.

Doing, then, is basically a wrapping or field of in–formation that conveys the experience of yourself as an active mind–body. This field comprises your mind and thinking, action and movement, tasks and events, and environment and context. All of those five things are constantly flowing and interacting. And you're part of that flowing whether you want it or not. At the same time, you can be aware and see that flow as a distinct observer and receiver of the experience coming through the field. This insight isn't a one–way street. When you learn to look and see with Modern Meditation, the link between Being and Doing opens up. Not only does your Doing mode perceive the world accurately (as opposed to functioning with clouded perception induced by thoughts and ego), but it also becomes illuminated by the inner light of your being – your observing Conscious Awareness. The day will light up for you as you fully express your true nature.

Reflective Moment

Use these journal prompts to support your growing insight.

Who are you?

At my core I am a field of pure conscious awareness. Which means:

Underneath my constantly changing body, thoughts and actions rests an unchanging inner conscious awareness that knows who I am and what I need to do.

*

I need not feel that I must keep working to stay in control. I can let go and enjoy moments of solitude and stillness – to just Be.

*

I know everything changes – nothing is fixed. Releasing this allows me to be free in the world and clearly see it all.

*

I can trust the world will support me and help me. All I need to do is let go, stop struggling, stay vigilant from the inside-out.

Chapter 7

WHERE ARE YOU?

'... we humans appear as particularly lively, intense, aware nodes of relation in an infinite network of connections, simple or complicated, direct or hidden, strong or delicate, temporary or very long-lasting.'

Ursula LeGuin

So far, so good, but how do you superimpose this new insight of inside/outside onto your daily experience and use it?

You might think, if I am directing my attention inward, what happens to the outside? Do I lose sight of where I am and what I'm doing? Conversely, if I am also trying to direct outward and inward attention, won't I get confused and muddled? It already sounds too hard!

Paradoxically, to change, you must stop and let go of the *imagined change* you think you want. Instead, open up to the real change you need, and it's flowing right here in the present moment. Luckily, this moment, the here and now, is constant and eternal, so you don't need to rush it, as you won't miss it if you are facing the right direction. Similarly, you don't need to go somewhere else to look for it. It's already here. This next step reveals where you are – where you have always been – right into the heart of the action.

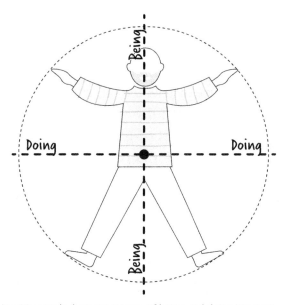

Figure 7: Where are You? Located where your sense of being and doing intersect.

On our evolving diagram, you can see I have given a name to each of the axes. The horizontal axis defines your **Doing** field. This is your realm of action and experience as you move on the planet's surface. This is the spatial and temporal world of events, where your life unfolds through the action you engage in.

Start by placing yourself in the centre of the diagram at the intersection of the two horizontal and vertical axes. At the intersection isn't only the portal to being your Self; it's you as mind and body. That's **where you are** and have been since the day you were born. To know that location requires learning to reorient yourself to it. That's key because without you as the observer, the creator and the participant using your increasingly refined and upgraded perception, the two axes or fields remain unknown. You have to be there. In fact, you are the there.

What's the Point? You Are!

I love Ursula LeGuin's insight that we are all *'aware nodes'* located right in the heart of the action, through which everything connects in an infinite web of possibilities. The web is fragile though because most of us are unaware of this bigger picture and its potential for support and change already built into the system. Modern Meditation will lift you out of this limited viewpoint, and when observed, everything will change.

In my other career as an architect and urban master planner, I spent much time designing node points. In placemaking and town building, a node is an active space where people, traffic, money, information, culture, history, identity or other urban flowing events and forces merge. Traditionally, a node point would be a spatial concentration, like a street intersection, a public space, a key public building, a transport interchange, or where cultural, political or commercial uses would collect around a key place.

The most important aspect of a node is distinctiveness. A place that would help establish a sense of location, place, legibility and meaning. A place people could *read* and feel and, from there, have an intimate and intuitive sense of how to locate themselves with connection and meaning. That's exactly what you're doing in these shifts. Using the four 'A's, you establish yourself as a node point – a point of meaning and purpose through which everything useful happens.

This is where you are. You are nowhere else. But realising this fully is all down to where and how you place your **Attention** – the first Modern Meditation skill you will cultivate. Understanding this is the start of you getting fully involved in the flow of your life as it really is.

Look and Then See

This shift becomes apparent when you discover how to look and see the world. Not everyone knowingly participates in this web of connection. It's invisible to most unless you know how to pay attention in a particular way – this is where Modern Meditation techniques come in.

This shift to, *Where Are You?* is an invitation to build a distinction in your mind between Doing and Being. Knowing the fields in this way is central to the shift of perception required.

Start by reading everything in the Doing field as an 'object'. An object is anything that *appears* to your senses and is processed through your thinking and experienced in your awareness – which means everything that you can see, touch, feel, name, etc. An object is also an event, an action, a place, a thought, an emotion, a sensation, etc. For example, your neighbour's new car, or your friend's smartphone, they're all objects. But your thoughts and feelings about your neighbour's new car or your friend's smartphone are objects too, and they attach together into a chain stretching inside and out.

Every object is in constant flux in itself and each other, interacting in a causal matrix. This is the material world of cause, effect and potential, where nothing is fixed. Even at the quantum or cosmic level, we know the observable, measurable world of Doing is a flowing and vibrating matrix. It's interesting to note here that the term *matrix* is also related to the word *matter* and linked to the Sanskrit word for Mother – *matr*. So by extension, we can say that everything in the Doing field is simply *Mother Nature at work.*

Equate this horizontal dimension with where you are now. You're reading this page, looking at the diagram. You are sitting, breathing, and holding the book or an e-reader. Expand your attention for a moment and see the space around you. The room where you're sitting has not always been there and will likely not be there in the future. In the universe's life, the room, you and the book just appear and disappear as a series of passing moments. Even if you see the room, you are in right now as pretty much fixed, it isn't. In terms of material and structure, it's in constant movement. In fact, on the quantum level, it's hardly there as it repeatedly shifts in and out of existence, moving between wave and particle, according to your observation. [16]

Now take your inner **Being** field and extend it as a vertical dimension. This is the same track that we defined in figure 7. This is you turning your attention inwards. When it crosses the Doing axis, you are bringing Doing and Being together. In other words, here is the moment when your attention is fully linked to where you are and what you are doing. This intersection is your node point of stillness against all the flow and flux.

_____

16. Ananthaswamy, A. 'What Does Quantum Theory Tell US About the Nature of Reality?' *Scientific American.* September 3, 2018. https://blogs.scientificamerican.com/observations/what-does-quantum-theory-actually-tell-us-about-reality/

Unifying the Fields

Where the Being and Doing fields intersect and merge into one, we can call this the 'Unified Field'. We don't create this field. It's always there. It's the source of everything, and when you learn to direct your attention in a particular way in Modern Meditation, you can see it, experience it, and even use it. And when you finally arrive there, it feels open, like a flowing momentum but simultaneously still and quiet.

> This intersection is your node point
> of stillness against all the flow and flux.

Don't see this Unified Field as something different or separate. It's YOU. It's you as pure expanded Conscious Awareness; it's you as the REAL you.

'The thing about meditation is: You become more and more you.'

David Lynch

When your attention is directed correctly, you will observe that Being and Doing occupy the same point – they are one and the same. But you will never know the truth unless you refine your perception and see and feel them that way. In fact, they are the same thing because they have to coexist. We realise the observed and the other the observer. More on this later.

Reflective Moment

Use these journal prompts to support your growing insight.

WHERE ARE YOU?

I exist and live fully at the point where my being and doing intersect and become one. This means:

I have unlimited access to wisdom, creativity, peace, energy and joy.

*

Knowing the permanence of my inner Self, my true sense of Being allows me to accept the change and flow of my outer world.

*

I know what to do at any given moment. Action is constant and always resolves itself. There is always a solution and a way forwards.

Chapter 8

WHEN ARE YOU?

'The Self is obscured by the world in order that the reality of both may be discovered. It is ignorance of our real nature that causes the Self to obscured.'

Effortless Being,
The Yoga Sutras of Patanjali, translated by Alistair Shearer

The second step, 'Where Are You?' invited you to locate right at the heart of the axes –where Being and Doing merge.

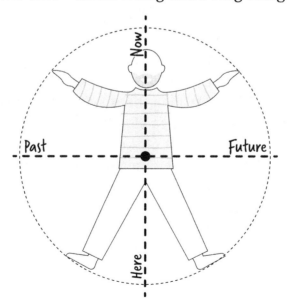

Figure 8: When are You? Located in the here and now.

In this next step, I have added new values to the diagram. The horizontal Doing axis is now marked 'past' and 'future', while the vertical Being axis is marked 'here' and 'now'. Your Doing field is temporal because it's your material world, but your sense of Being has nothing to do with time. So when the two axes cross at your conscious node point, you are totally present in what is as it flows. Look closely at this point. Feel it. It's the answer to When Are You?

But it's more than that. Because you are the **NOW**. Without you to observe, the NOW doesn't exist. For some, this is precisely what is missing in life – the NOW has gone missing in action.

Right Here and Right Now.

Only NOW is Real

This is always a difficult concept in our **beanddo** training because, for many people, their thinking mind only knows how to be in the future or past. Their mind-body attaches to thoughts that continually travel backwards and forwards, trying to hopelessly resolve situations that have happened or might not happen. For many, the idea of being present is an unknown experience. Many spend most of their time and energy attaching to mental dramas playing out as **what-if** and **what-was**. There is hardly ever **what-is** going on. Imagine how much of life, which is and can only ever be **what is**, in the NOW, is being missed.

Why Now?

Often in my classes, people say, 'But it's the **NOW** I'm trying to escape from. My life is a real struggle at the moment!'

This is part of the challenge. Ask yourself – *Is what I am anxious and fearful about actually happening right now?* The answer is invariably no! It hardly ever is the case. And there is a good reason to know that what you are actually worrying about won't actually happen anyway. So the suffering you are experiencing right now is only because your brain and nervous system can't tell the difference between *what is* and *what if*. What happens then is your self-defence mechanism; your flight/flight activates regardless of what is happening. This is why those who suffer this way can easily *think* themselves into a panic attack. I know. I used to be great at it. Your body is flooded with adrenaline and cortisol, keeping you tense and hypervigilant. This is okay when there is a real threat, but not on Sunday evening when you are getting ready for work in the morning. So for many people, unresolved actions in response to fight/flight eventually evolve into constant and generalised anxiety and dread.

It's Okay

But it's okay to suffer. Don't ever see your pain as a failure. In fact, it can be the only time we really get to grow. Suffering is a message that says, 'change' – **Be** different and **Do** differently. You don't need to be that ideal, imagined person you think you should be. That is certainly my experience.

'Forget your perfect offering. There is a crack in everything, that's how the light gets in.'

Leonard Cohen

Show me someone who hasn't suffered in life, and I will show you an individual that is perhaps asleep, lacking in compassion, creativity and imagination. They have learned next to nothing from a very limited life experience. After all, the world's complexities, challenges and joys are designed to give you the experience to help you know who you are. The world demands you pay attention to it and align with its momentum in a way that allows you to learn.

There is a good reason why some people have difficulty being present. Because in the NOW, all thinking naturally slows down or stops, which feels scary to those who live in their heads. Thoughts can't get purchase in the present because they are linked to the past or future.

The NOW has nothing to do with time. It's an eternal moment – right here, right now. It's often said in yogic science that whoever knows the NOW knows everything and is free. This is because being in the NOW changes how the mind works. It opens you up and sharpens your perception, putting you in the heart of the flow of things as they are. From there, you can make powerful insights and collaborate with the best and most appropriate action.

What Is the Present Moment?

Even though the horizontal dimension marks a past and

future, they are only there to help define the now – the point where what you are doing externally merges and intersects with internal Conscious Awareness. Remember, when we take Conscious Action like this, time doesn't define us. We are in the moment. How long is a moment? Well, there is no beginning or end. It's a constant.

'Ultimately, all moments are really one, therefore now is an eternity.'

David Bohm

And because the moment is located right where you are linked to your awareness, you realise there are no divisions between you, where you are and what you are doing.

In other words, being fully present in the Now is constant and boundless, permeating everything, and upgrading how you see, feel, hear and **Do**. An experienced meditator will tell you that thoughts, clock time defined by your timesheet, watch or smartphone, don't exist. When you start flowing with Conscious Action, everything is in the NOW. This insight will help you be very productive. Deadlines still exist, of course, but the stress and fear of not making them fall away. You'll find you will always have enough time.

If you spend time running over an imagined future event that you desperately want or don't want to happen, your attention will travel unconsciously along the horizontal line towards the future (wherever that is) and away from your node point. This is you trying to mentally shape and change the future before it happens, which is impossible. Only in the NOW at the intersection point can you actually change anything. Conversely, if your attention habitually slides in the other direction, towards the past, you find yourself running over past events, again trying to change and reset them to better fit a more comforting narrative in the hope that you feel better in the NOW. Again, your attention slips away from the intersection point.

Things That Don't Exist

When your attention is sliding habitually backwards and forwards along the horizontal dimension, you identify with things that don't exist. You shift away from what's real and the world becomes distorted by imagined expectations, aversions, attachments and wants. Daily life becomes a mental struggle as you try to *think* your wants and aversions into reality.

This leads to problems that seem particularly 21st century, but it's always been the case. For example, if your attachment is linked to past objects (thoughts), then invariably, feelings of guilt, regret and depression arise in the now. Conversely, if you are attached to the outcome of future events, this leads to anxiety and fear. Aversion, expectation or attachment to imagined outcomes are the primary sources of unhappiness. Your knowledge of the past and future is a story you tell yourself in the present because it's based on your perception of the events. And here is the challenge. When you locate yourself at the node, you are in the present moment of intersection. This means with practise, you can watch and even stand away from the drama habitually unfolding in your head. So stay here in the present, where things are happening. Modern Meditation will help you achieve that.

Reflective Moment

Use these journal prompts to support your growing insight.

WHEN ARE YOU?

I am right here right now. It's impossible to be anywhere else. Which means:

Only now is it real. Only in the now can I make real and lasting change.

*

Right here, right now I am doing exactly what I planned to do.

*

I set expectations that are reasonable and accept fully whatever happens.

*

I am not in the now, I am the NOW.

Chapter 9

WHAT ARE YOU?

'You come into this world with nothing, and you go empty-handed. The wealth of life lies in how you allow its experience to enrich you.'

Sadhguru

The first three shifts were a prelude to understanding how and why Modern Meditation works and why you need to make the unconscious conscious.

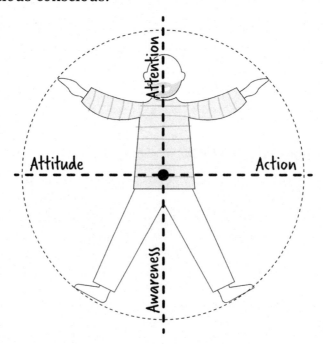

Figure 9: What are You? A matrix of attention, awareness attitude and action alive in the world.

Step 1 introduced the realisation that you have an internal and external life – two fields of operation, **Being** and **Doing**, through which information flows. Most of the time, the potential from their conscious unity is hardly fulfilled. They are never allowed to consciously coincide because many of us live in a distracted, habitual subconscious reaction to the world. We go through the motions without paying attention.

Step 2 then invited you to see this duality in the context of your daily life. We defined Doing as a horizontal dimension, which defined you in action, feeling and thinking as you move around the planet's surface. While Being was defined as an inward, vertical engagement with your deeper reality.

Step 3 then invited you to become present, to occupy the here and now. This is the space, event or moment where the two axes intersect – where Being and Doing merge into a single point. This is where you need to maintain your attention. This is where you need to live. Each shift is principally an invitation to direct your attention in a particular way to increasingly upgrade and attune your cognition, senses, outlooks and thoughts.

Now we open up to **step 4**. You can see that I have refined the values again. The horizontal axis, the Doing field, is defined by **Attitude** at one end and **Action** at the other. While the vertical Being dimension is marked by **Attention** at the top and **Awareness** at the bottom. These are the meditation skills which you'll cultivate to locate and establish yourself at the constant conscious node point.

What you are in the world, in terms of knowing your authentic, conscious Self, is determined by how you use these four essential cognitions. For example, ask yourself:

- How much **attention** do I actually pay to my actions, others and the wider world, or am I more distracted by what is going on in my head?

- How **aware** am I of what is happening and what is actually needed?

- Is the world a disappointment because I shape it solely by my **attitude?**

- And are most of the **actions** I undertake pointless, unhelpful and exhausting?

Even though you are looking at the skills individually, they are integral. They are connected because using these skills together is a cyclical process of experiencing, observing, thinking and acting. Modern Meditation is an integrated procedure; each part of the cycle is co-dependent. Each **A** is an inner cognitive skill developed through Modern Meditation. In short, we'll focus not on the content of each **A** but directly on the process.

You are going to *perceive* **the process of Attention and Awareness** and *process* **how you perceive Attitude and Action.**

This means:

- **Attention** is modified towards a continuous, direct focus on an internal/external object/task or experience at hand.

- **Awareness** is modified towards an inner reflective orientation, where your sense of place, moment and action becomes internalised.

- **Attitude** is modified towards an unconditioned observation and acceptance with minimised expectation or interference.

- **Action** is modified towards flowing engagement and complete absorption, with whatever task is underway without exception.

The point is to practise these cognitions until they feel like a *continuum*. Something present and self-sustaining.

Perception and Processing

Remember, at the start of this book, I defined meditation as a 'change of perspective'. The practice involves a modified shift in perception and processing that activates a deeper reality of who you are, what you're for and what you can do.

Remember also, I said you only have to cultivate two skills,

1. Change the way you perceive information.
2. Change the way you process information.

Now let's start testing it.

In Figure 10, you can see I have added these new insights to give a full picture of the practice. You can also see that the vertical Being field axis is referred to as your *perception continuum*, and the horizontal Doing field axis is referred to as your *processing continuum*.

Figure 10: Perception and processing continuum.

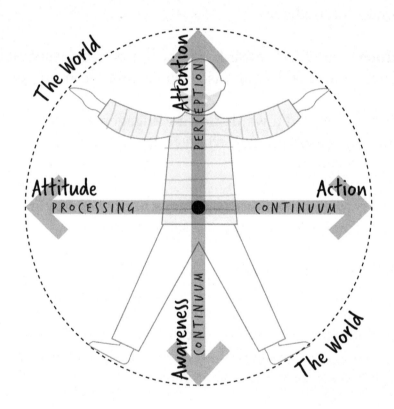

The Being Field Axis – Perception Continuum

Starting with the Being axis field, the vertical dimension is marked by *Attention* at the top and *Awareness* at the bottom. It's on this line that you will shift perception and bring **Attention** to **Awareness**. Linked by a **continuum of perception**, it refers to how *Attention* and *Awareness* mix and merge, creating a continuous flowing method of perception. Here, your attention is primarily inwards by actively cultivating the merging of Attention and Awareness into an overall practice. When you see and occupy this field, no matter how intermittently, you move towards a sense of being as a field of consciousness. You then practice Attention and Awareness skills, so they combine and maintain constant contact with what is, as real-time information flowing along the horizontal Doing field not only through your direct perception but also through knowing insight.

This shift is just the start.

The Doing Field Axis – Processing Continuum

Intersecting with the processing continuum is where you bring a new type of *Attitude* to *Action*. The aim here is to maintain a connection to the field of experience, to nurture and *hold* these episodes of heightened awareness, not only in your formal practice but also in everyday life.

As you occupy this field, you are open to a momentary insight, a unifying wholeness described earlier. Here the *subject* – you as the experiencer and observer in the Being field – collapses and combine into every *object* as they pass through your perception inside the Doing field. At one end of the continuum, awareness takes the form of highly attuned sensing or intuition, where you feel full contact with the flow of what is happening. And where your attention is perfected, remaining undistracted and directed to maintain the awareness experience.

Your awareness will grow naturally due to carefully directed Modern Meditation Attention. Attention itself on purpose, for purpose, is a required skill that needs to be practised, without which cultivated awareness is impossible.

By strengthening your Attention and holding it into Awareness, you grow this field into one overall powerful moment. Regular Modern Meditation practice allows you to notice not only this experience of conscious empowerment but also when it disappears. It's here you become aware of just how much you are getting in the way of yourself, and in particular, how attachment to your thinking impacts how you process and see the world around us. This discovery is a great moment for many meditators and is the start of taking conscious control.

So when you learn to pay **Attention** in a particular way, supported by a particular **Attitude** of observation, you nurture a deeper **Awareness** which impacts the quality of your experience *and* **Action** – in other words, cultivate Conscious Action. This is where you naturally begin to access deeper capacities and possibilities.

So as you begin to refine your perception along the **vertical perception continuum – Attention + Awareness** you will see its impacts on the qualities of your horizontal continuum where your **Attitude** opens to limitless possibilities and **Action** becomes effortless, light and easy – you FLOW. When you become skilled in this 'insight' (and it is *inner sight*, a place to observe and act in the world), you cultivate the skills required for your Doing, the processing continuum where Conscious Action happens.

> This is a place of full coherence,
> where consciousness becomes an intention,
> an idea, and insight and action.

Follow the steps, and the practice will take you to the heart of this insight. This is a place of full coherence, where consciousness becomes an intention, an idea, and insight and action. A place where anything is possible but...

1. What sort of Attention?
2. What sort of Awareness?
3. What sort of Attitude?
4. What sort of Action?

We will explore these four Modern Meditation skills in Part III.

Reflective Moment

Use these journal prompts to support your growing insight.

WHAT ARE YOU?

I am an instrument of infinite flowing potential, creativity and joy. Which means:

I can remain engaged, attentive and centred whatever events and experiences and actions flow through me.

*

It's impossible to feel empty, useless and lost. Being conscious in action means being whole, purposeful and effective.

*

Right here, right now, I am doing exactly what I planned to do.

PART TWO

PART THREE
THE FOUR 'A'S OF MODERN MEDITATION

'When the mind has settled, we are established in our essential nature, which is unbounded Consciousness.'

~ *Effortless Being, The Yoga Sutras of Patanjali, translated by Alistair Shearer*

Chapter 10

STRATEGIES FOR DEVELOPING CONSCIOUS ATTENTION

"The more a man knows about himself in relation to every kind of experience, the greater his chance of suddenly, one fine morning, realising who in fact he is..."

Aldous Huxley, Island

One of my earlier Swami teachers often reminded us; *Attention leads to Awareness. Awareness leads to Meditation. Meditation leads to Joy. But it starts with Attention!'* Cultivating attention is your first Modern Meditation practice. Attention is everything. It's vital, because without engagement and perfecting this skill, nothing else is possible.

You Are Here!

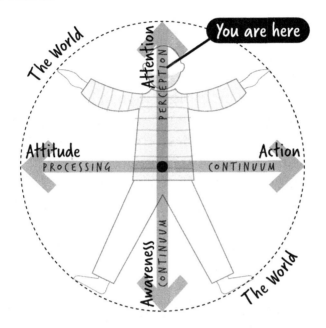

Figure 11: Developing conscious attention.

To evolve from mostly unconscious reactions to Conscious Action and see ourselves, others and the world in a whole new way, then we have to learn to *pay Attention.* This is the moment where we learn to reposition against those habitual, tiring and painful self-created mental and emotional objects that so often fuel our unconscious default reactivity. At the end of this section, you'll find a simple Modern Meditation Attention Practice. It's designed to help you open up towards a shift from a thinking, analysing mind to a sensing, seeing and knowing mind. Treat it as an introduction and a way into the whole practice.

When you learn to pay attention, on purpose, for its own sake, you'll likely be surprised at how much time and energy you waste and how much unhappiness and anger you create for yourself and others. You'll discover your attention as a *thing* is either switched off or, more likely, continually attached to something that doesn't ultimately serve your wellbeing. In Aldous Huxley's last book, *Island*, he described a yoga paradise called 'Pala', where the indigenous Mynah birds on the island, with their ability to mimic human voices, were trained to call *'attention'* and *'here and now'*. Seen through the experience of the main protagonist, a cynical journalist called Will Farnaby, he asks: *'Why 'Attention'? Why 'Here and now?'* And is answered: *"That's what you always forget, isn't it? I mean, you forget to pay attention to what's happening. And that's the same as not being here and now."*

> You'll be using attention not as a way of cataloguing or judging what you look at but as a way of knowing and witnessing what you see.

What Are You Going to Pay Attention to?

You, inside and out, located here and now, but not in a judgemental, narcissistic way. This new Attention skill doesn't look outwards for things to be resolved or compared. This is paying Attention to the NOW through you as you are, without interference. Cultivating this new skill moves your Attention inwards behind thoughts, feelings, senses and actions, and into the source of Attention. You'll be using Attention not as a way of cataloguing or judging what you *look* at but as a way of *knowing* and *witnessing* what you see.

We know that human attention is a narrow resource. Unlike Awareness, which we will look at next, it seems we only direct our Attention in a limited way to one thing at a time. For example, if you want to read this page fully, your Attention cannot be invested, for the moment, anywhere else. Yet your Attention can be easily switched and manipulated away from what you are doing. Our Attention span (in the digital world) is now thought to be less than two seconds, so for those who want to distract you, it's very easy. The amount of apps, services, adverts, products and news competing for your limited Attention bandwidth is a testament to that.

Your Attention can jump away or be redirected without you even noticing or become attached to a whole sequence of passing objects. Great for magicians, advertising executives, social media giants and politicians. Not so good if you want to live a conscious life in the present. These distractions that grab our Attention are *sense objects*, in that it is the senses that Attention uses to attach. Sense objects can take many forms. The most powerful and overwhelming thing is that *object* of a passing thought, as they appear everywhere, every moment, by themselves. These objects will fully occupy us and change how the world appears.

However, limited Attention can be useful. When you learn to attend and hold on to one singular object, all other objects or distractions tend to fade away. This aspect of Attention is useful for meditation as you begin to use your Attention skills as a prelude for cultivating deeper awareness. I'm not talking about concentration. That's different. Concentration is about focusing, labelling, categorising and memorising one thing compared to another. Concentration comes with tension. Instead, Modern Meditation cultivates *unsanctioned* and *unconditional Attention*. It takes skill to maintain Attention like this, but ironically little effort. Because you will learn to *gently* direct your Attention differently. It's a mind–body practice, not the type of hard focus and concentration you probably learned at school, designed to *take in* information to make it stick and gain some advantage. That way of teaching Attention to pass examinations is so 20th Century. We are going to learn a more useful way of paying Attention.

Ironically, the key to this type of Attention is *inattention*. After a while, you will begin to notice where your Attention goes. You will notice when your directed Attention begins to warp, jump and bend towards something else. And it will happen constantly. But don't give up. Ask yourself who or what is doing the noticing? The answer is YOU as Conscious Awareness. So the more you notice, the more you are conscious, helping you get some balance over your 95/5 default mental state.

What's Happened to Attention?

From the moment we are born, we are plunged into a world of words, ideas, concepts, beliefs, and do's and don'ts. More than ever, we are shaped by cultural and social filters in an increasingly subdivided and fragmented world. I always find it strange when people say I was born Christian, Mormon or Hindu etc... How do they know? They were born human first and foremost. All the labels, filters, divisions and classifications come later, when human–made identities to support certain social and cultural views of the world were applied by others.

Because of this lifelong conditioning, almost all of us spend much time paying Attention to what is happening in our heads rather than what is happening around us. We're in a constant state of mental distraction, connected to thoughts and thinking, confusing them for the facts we believe underpin reality.

In some ways, we now live in an Attention illiterate world. We have lost the skills and don't know how to pay Attention on purpose, for purpose. This has worsened since the advent of the internet and social media, which has worked out a way of monetising our attention. Our Attention is constantly filtered and interfered with. We rarely see the world as it is, others or ourselves as we are. Before long, we can think that we see, hear, touch, feel and not bother with reality. When that happens, the Being and Doing of life will disappear completely.

The 'Attention Economy', as it's called, is the business that makes money out of our Attention. But to do that, they need to develop more sophisticated ways of attracting, holding and manipulating our Attention to sell us something that we probably don't actually need or convince us something is real to serve a wider political purpose. To direct and hold your attention, the idea is to stimulate unconscious reactivity in your default mode, which simultaneously activates the stress hormones. The result scrolling mindlessly through your phone to keep the addictive chemicals flowing.

Controlling and holding your Attention to monetise it happens like this:

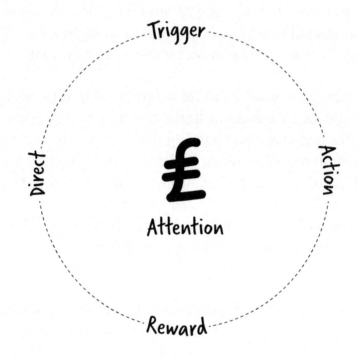

Figure 12: Attention monetisation trigger.

Trigger

A trigger is the starting point of the Attention monetisation process. The trigger is designed to make us want (via a little hit of cortisol) something that we think we need. If the trigger is shaped effectively, it *switches on* our inbuilt sense of lack.

Action

We are then *called to action* (a little hit of adrenaline) because we are told that opening that application, selecting that product, and looking at that post will be the opportunity to ease the emptiness.

Reward
Then attention is fixed and held momentarily as we earn self-gratification (a little dopamine hit), by whatever our manipulated Attention discovers.

Direct
Then finally, the money-making step of the Attention monetisation process. Here, as the dopamine shot recedes, our Attention is shifted to the carefully placed and designed adjacent advert, and the process starts again.

And the advertising industry rewards people for this work!

And what fuels the whole money-making cycle is the carefully designed manipulation of your default, habitual unconscious reaction. Generators of the Attention Economy want you to stay locked unconsciously inside your default mode with no way out! The last thing they want you to do is to *notice* this and become conscious and free, although ironically, that's what they tell you will be if you buy whatever is being promoted. In fact, the more intense your default mode, the more extreme the habits that are giving rise to addiction, which are the most profitable. Just look at how gambling on the internet has thrived. Emotions and fears are also exploited. FOMO marketing (fear of missing out) directly influences your ego-based tendencies. Fear is the operative word. In other words, your fight-flight-freeze response is deliberately switched on, forcing yet another unconscious reaction. People trapped inside this cycle live in a constantly heightened sense of dread and anxiety.

Putting you back in charge so you can cultivate your attention on purpose will lift you out of this depressing cycle if you're in it. Once you learn to *see* this manipulative and life-limiting process, it will break. You can see it's all about unconscious attachment. With Modern Meditation techniques focused on Conscious Action, you discover you have a choice not to get attached.

How to Pay Attention?

What are we paying Attention to? Everything and anything, in other words, the NOW. **What** we pay Attention to, in the form of objects or in-formation, isn't that important. The whole world is there for you to practice meditation on. It's **how** you pay Attention. That is key here, which means starting with you, who you are, where you are and what you are doing.

So here is the first skill you need to master – directing your attention with purpose.

You are not paying Attention to in-formation to interfere with it, build on it, judge or process. This Attention is softer, smarter and open. You will now be in **receive mode**, a witness to the world, as in-formation in flux and flow, in real-time. This means, of course, working with your **senses**, but in a very conscious and deliberate way. You won't be closing them off. Instead, you will open them up. Whatever you feel, see, hear, taste, smell, think and know can flow into awareness without interference or judgement. The key here is to bring your Attention to your senses when they receive the flux of in-formation. You do this by locating yourself *behind* each of your senses. You are *watching* each sense pick up and deliver information. Don't worry if this shift of perception seems impossible. It isn't it's just a shift of attitude which will come with practice. This is paying Attention to paying Attention. You will soon discover your Attention will gradually morph into awareness, the next cognitive skill on the vertical perceptual field axis.

In this way, you naturally embrace **what is** in the moment because your senses only work in the present. So the information flowing is NOW the point from which Awareness grows.

> The information flowing is NOW
> the point from which Awareness grows.

Developing Your New Attention Skills

A good example here is the difference between looking and seeing. When we look at something, we invariably interfere with what we are looking at. We create a mental filter that asks: *What am I looking at? What am I expected to know? Seeing* is when we do know. All labels and questions just disappear to reveal the deeper reality of what is being seen. The space between the observer and the observed diminishes, while at the same time, a sense of space emerges that seems to contain everything. This is paying Attention to **what is** – the world's reality – not what others have told you, and it's a vital insight to feel and use. Here is a good example. Next time you find yourself at a museum or gallery, train yourself to *see* first and *look* second. By that, I mean resist reading the explanatory label located near the art piece or artefact until whatever you are observing speaks back to you. You don't need to start knowing by thinking about words, dates, ideas and concepts written on that little piece of card. It will tell you nothing.

When you direct your Attention like this, you won't see a painting there – you are actually looking back at yourself in full receptive harmony with the world right there. That's what the world is for.

Cultivating Conscious Attention

Our first **A** practice, ATTENTION, is a type of *somatic* exercise designed to help you switch on your attention, direct and hold for increasingly longer periods. Treat this as a steppingstone or threshold into the whole practice.

The first thing is to sit, be still, and give yourself a moment to settle into where you are and what you are doing. Adopt a comfortable posture, close your mouth and breathe through your nose. No analysis is required. Switch off expectations and simply feel your way through the technique. There is no wrong or right way to do this.

Then you will simply direct your attention softly towards the experience of being in the body and what it's doing for you right now. The intention is to direct attention unconditionally to a particular part of the body. Your body will respond to your attention via a soft internal radiant or buzzing, heat, lightness, heaviness or flowing energy sensation.

This simple opening practice connects your mind and body, eventually leading to a deeper embodied experience. The sensation responds to your attention – *you don't need to force it*. The sensation is useful because when it disappears, you will know that your Attention has, most likely and unknowingly, attached to a passing thought or distraction. To cultivate

Attention, the intention is to maintain and *hold* the *felt sensation* and, after some practice, purposefully guide it across your whole body. The sensation combines your nervous system and subtle energy body responding to your Conscious Attention.

We start with the body because meditation is a whole mind-body practice, as your body is the only part of you in the present moment. We start with fingers and toes, as the extremities are particularly sensitive to this practice. There is also a small intention setting too. Learn this and use it often, even in your formal practice, but also while doing the laundry. Tell yourself mentally:

- I am exactly where I planned to be.

- I am doing exactly what I planned to do.

- There is nowhere else to be. There is nothing else to do. This is it. Only **now** is real.

PART THREE

MODERN MEDITATION FOR ATTENTION PRACTICE

1. *Choose an upright chair and settle in for the moment. Be comfortable. Relax and feel your body in the chair. Feel its position, its shape, and its posture as you sit. Feel your back on the chair, your feet on the floor. Feel your hands resting palm up in your lap.*

2. *With your eyes softly closed or eyelids lowered, bring your Attention to the fingers of your left hand. Don't move your fingers. Just feel them with your Attention. Be aware of them. After a while, you will feel a gentle vibrancy. A subtle humming or buzzing in your fingers. When you notice, stay with it. Notice how the depth and momentum of the vibrancy are linked to your Attention. It might come and go. It might have a wave-like form. Just stay with whatever you are feeling. It's fine as it is.*

3. *Now without letting go of the Attention on the fingers of your left hand, expand your Attention to your right hand. Notice how the vibrant sensation flows across both hands, deeply linked to your Attention. Try to sustain the sensation across them both.*

4. *Now without losing your Attention on your fingers and hands, expand your Attention to your toes. First, the left and then the right toes. Again try to sustain the vibration by maintaining your Attention where needed.*

5. *Now you have four points of connection. You have four coordinates to position yourself within your body, in this space, at this moment.*

6. *Stay with it. If the vibrancy has fallen away, it's only because the mind-body connection has been broken as your attention wanders. Simply bring it back to reconnect and stay with it.*

7. *After a while, you might begin to feel a little more relaxed. Stay with this feeling, as this indicates you are falling into the present. Without too much effort, use your attention to guide that vibrancy up through your arms into your chest and upper body.*

8. *Without too much effort, use your Attention to guide that vibrancy up through your legs and into your lower body and then allow your Attention now to open up across your whole body. Feel that vibrancy, that deep sense of aliveness flow through your body.*

9. *Don't worry if there are areas that feel blocked or don't respond. That's normal. Just go where your mind and body let you go. Just flow. As you feel the whole body, a deeper feeling of relaxation emerges. There is an openness, maybe a dropping inside, a softening or mellowing. A comforting feeling of just being. Letting go. Don't resist it. Allow it to come through. Stay with that feeling, but don't define or grab it. Don't own it. Just let it be as it is.*

10. *After a while, you'll experience a feeling of spaciousness. Openness. Your body feels light, open, not bound by outside or inside. Just a knowing, spacious feeling of presence. Again, if your mind wanders, simply bring it back to that experience. Don't be critical. Just notice and then bring it back. Notice what you need to do to maintain that space and how you have shaped your Attention towards knowing that feeling?*

Daily Conscious Attention Strategies

As your ability to direct and pay Attention enhances, you will discover that everything is worthy of your Attention. Paying deep Attention in this way will sharpen the day. Remember, however, to pay Attention gently and not be compulsive about this in some unhealthy or attached way. You are not trying to fix anything, force or manage anything. You are simply watching. Watching the flow of your actions in space, your speech and thoughts. Watching your body breathe and feel. Watching the wind in the trees, the grass growing, the birds flying, the world turning. It's all in-formation happening all by itself. By paying Attention like this, it's easier to see all actions as Conscious Action, as they seem to emerge from a higher state of Being and Doing and not mere habit.

1. Pay Attention
Focus on everything you do while your body and mind are in action. Observe your actions. Watch while using your body, hands, arms, legs, thoughts, feelings etc. You are in action all of the time.

2. Be in Control
Choose where and how to direct your Attention rather than the Attention being pulled by distraction. Observe your senses, noticing that smelling, tasting, seeing, touching, and hearing are all happening.

3. Manage the Process
Inattention is key. Notice when your Attention jumps from where you are and what you're doing into the inner mental

world of distractions. This will often happen, requiring constant self-management.

4. Be Aware
Frequently bring your Attention to your breathing and the quality of the breath. Notice how this helps you to see and be aware of your thinking process and emotions.

5. Observe
Notice and observe the stillness and silence within, not only externally but also your internal states.

Regular practice results in upgraded life experiences and improved daily outcomes. For example:

- You will notice when and where your Attention has wandered, prompting you to bring it back purposefully.

- You will notice moments when the thinking, describing and judging mind shifts to a sensing and knowing mind.

- You will feel more connected to the senses and the body as the primary vehicle for experiencing being present.

- You will discover the vital skill of self-starting periods of purposeful calm and relaxation from the inside out.

Affirmation

I am an instrument of infinite flowing change and potential. All I need to do is get out of my own way.

Chapter 11

STRATEGIES FOR DEVELOPING CONSCIOUS AWARENESS

'Awareness is not a matter of determination. Awareness is the silent and choiceless observation of what is; in this awareness the problem unrolls itself, and thus it is fully and completely understood.'

Jiddu Krishnamurti

Now we move along the vertical axis towards **Awareness**. Having got to grips with directed **Attention** at one end, you are in a good position to go further and deeper into where your Attention is taking you – a deeper innate agency and insight over how you think, feel and behave.

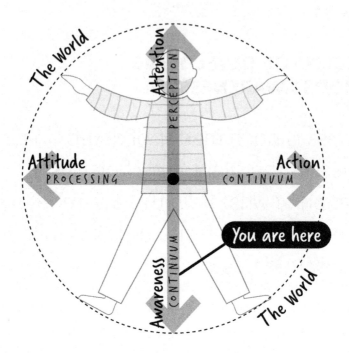

Figure 13: Developing conscious awareness.

There is a simple Modern Meditation Awareness Practice at the end of this section to help you open up towards a shift of cognition that will point to a deeper, more spatial experience of who and what you are. Awareness is the pivotal interface between your inner and outer worlds. It's also the constant operating principle that keeps them in unison. Being Aware is like waking up. You see the whole thing at last. Awareness is a resource that never runs out. In fact, it's like love – it's effortless – the more you use, the more you get, and the more you understand how things work.

You can't force yourself into Awareness. That's impossible. You can, however, discover how to occupy a space in which

Awareness grows and unfolds naturally. This suggests that your sense of Awareness is a deeper state of being which is always present. The opening quote from Krishnamurti nicely explains why those people with limited self-awareness (and there are plenty of them, mostly in positions of power and authority), who have never discovered how to occupy a deeper attitude, make so many misjudgements about themselves, others and the world.

People who lack awareness or insight will often suffer from the Dunning-Kruger Effect. [17] These people are monumentally incompetent at what they do but are too incompetent to realise. Determined to believe and convince others they are gifted experts, their ego trio 'I, Me and Mine' are so powerful they operate inside an illusionary world of personal success, entitlement and expectation. They are everywhere, in governments, in business, the media and in your community. In a world where we need to promote more creativity, leadership and compassion, they are on the wrong side of history.

What Is Awareness?

Awareness is what's left when all the thinking, wanting, expectation, labelling and planning end. Awareness comes with feelings of wellbeing, wholeness and joy that simply rise inside you. You'll know this because it's where your creativity, compassion and empathy come. The closer you get to this source of you, the better you will feel as a more effective version of you emerges.

---

17. Kruger, J., & Dunning, D. 'Unskilled and unaware of it: How difficulties in recognizing one's own incompetence lead to inflated self-assessments', Journal of Personality and Social Psychology, 1999; 77(6), 1121-1134. https://doi.org/10.1037/0022-3514.77.6.1121

It's a good idea here to remember the first shift I used in
Chapter 6 as Modern Meditation when practised properly as a
'non-dual' or 'unitive' practice that leads to innate moments
of 'oneness'. In other words, you reach a state where all your
ideas, decisions and actions are based on seeing the world
clearly, shaped and defined by the inner realm of Conscious
Awareness of Being.

I mentioned earlier that one of the shifts required for a liberated
life is to realise you are *not your thoughts* as there is something
more fundamental to your reality. This is one of the most
important aspects of Modern Meditation. To be fully aware,
then, is to live, work, play and love as pure consciousness as
the creator, recipient and witness of all that is happening.
This self-realisation comes down to the single question, who
or what is experiencing? Are you, on the surface, a judging,
labelling individual or something deeper and more fundamental
altogether?

You will discover that Awareness as a felt experience is spatial,
boundless and starts as an internal condition. When you learn
how to hold and inhabit that inner spatial awareness, you can
access higher capacities of connection and perception. You will
find that you begin to move more effortlessly, and the world
appears sharper and more immediate. Things seem to emerge
with meaning and intention, no matter how small or irrelevant
you might think they are. Even the smallest actions and events
in your daily life have depth and dimension.

After a while, you'll notice that inside that Awareness space,
everything you experience is interconnected events. Everything,
including your actions, body and feelings, seems to flow in a

conscious self-organised pattern. They come and go. Nothing is fixed but at the same time, full of possibility and potential. And there, right in the centre of this flow, is You. When you learn to nurture this deeper Awareness, everything that happens, you realise, has meaning and purpose. But don't stress here. You don't need to look for this sense of purpose; this deeper dimension will come to you without effort, *'unmasked'* as Franz Kafka described earlier (see page 92). All you need to do is locate and inhabit that field of deep stillness and silent Conscious Awareness. It means that you have woken up to the reality of things and actually exist in a different, brighter world. A world that nobody ever told was there, located only a moment away.

In your Modern Meditation practice, you begin to see it's impossible to split these two A's – *Awareness is a function of Attention, and Attention is a function of Awareness.* In your Attention practice, you use your mind-body to acknowledge the flow of in-formation as it comes and goes. You are in receive mode only. So what or who is aware of this raw data as it flows through your senses? What or who is the receiver? – The answer is You as pure Conscious Awareness! And with practice, not only can you feel this, but you also align with this deeper part of you by learning how to observe through meditation.

The Observer

The more you practice Modern Meditation, the more you'll become familiar with *observing or witnessing what is happening in your internal and external world.* The very act of watching and witnessing without getting involved is Awareness – being aware of not only your thoughts and feelings but also your actions. It's here you start to shift towards Conscious Action.

To get a clearer picture of this new Awareness and get a feel for it, look at Figure 4 again. Your adaptive unconscious default mode is the mechanism of your day-to-day nature. But here, let's add a new component, a new cognition of the observer as *self-awareness* which is located right in the middle. Because Awareness is the space through which all in-formation flows and every action, thought, sensation and feeling are observed, it can't be readily located on the periphery as a part of the looping default mode. Its nature as innate or natural Awareness is distinct, separate and watches from the inside out. This aspect of Awareness is vital because the practice involves coming in behind your senses, actions and thoughts to *observe* everything as an object as they flow through Awareness as experience. We will look at how to do this later.

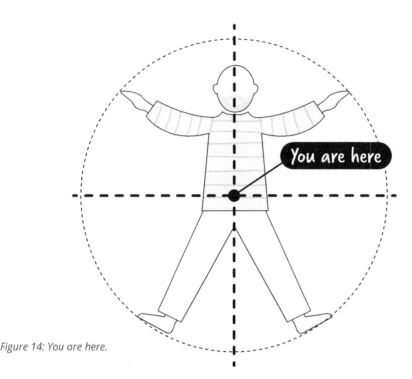

Figure 14: You are here.

Patanjali, the architect of modern yoga reminds us, *'when the mind has settled, we are established in our essential nature, which is unbounded Consciousness.'* So it's our thinking, or how we think about things, that divides us from being truly conscious of things as they are. Right now, you exist in an endless ocean of objects and things that come to life through your senses. In the same way, Being doesn't exist without Doing; Awareness cannot happen unless there is something to be aware of.

We live in a world of judgement. We confuse words with reality. The word isn't the thing at all. Just look at how this basic mistake of perception fuels the hate and toxicity in social media, where likes and dislikes, opinions, feelings, prejudice and critical judgement are frequently mistaken for fact. But what if you become aware of this conditioned response. Not just superficially aware of things but actually being aware without getting involved in all the other stuff as it plays out. This, then, is awareness nurtured with Modern Meditation practice that places you into a new, fully responsive, independent relationship with the world.

Practising Modern Meditation based observation towards any object without any psychological interference, you'll discover who the creator of division and separateness is. This is good news because, as Aldous Huxley said at the beginning of the book, all we need to do is work out a way of 'not getting in the way of our own light'. We don't need to do anything to be aware; just clear out all the stuff that blocks awareness and its deeper dimensions and find a space from which to observe.

Modern Meditation practice upgrades and expands perception and shifts our perspective. Not only do we see what makes us real to each other, but also the reality of the universe. Connections are everywhere when we experience the world, not as separate objects or things to be owned or controlled but as a flowing field of relationships and events where nothing is wasted. There is no product as such other than love.

'The tree which moves some to tears of joy is in the eyes of others only a green thing which stands in the way... As a man is, so he sees.'

William Blake

PART THREE

When real Awareness emerges, you begin meditating on
the world with your eyes open. Like your formal practice,
the distance between you as the observer and the observed
collapses into one singular experience. This brings your Modern
Meditation technique to everyday experience.

It's down to you to keep your Attention directed towards
Awareness. You might say your *Awareness is your core Self*. The
difference between me and not-me is that part who knows who
you are, where you are and what you are for. But it's down to
you to put that into action, remembering that we are all bound
by action all the time. I have talked a great deal about *human-
made traps*. You can remain unconsciously reactive and let others
create your world and trap you, or you can act consciously and
make the world real. It's down to you to make that choice.

'Nobody can push you out of your trap... All
that you have to do is to be aware from the
beginning to the end, not become inattentive
in the middle of it.'

J. Krishnamurti

Developing Your New Conscious Awareness Skills

Awareness, then, isn't self-induced because it's already there.
But you will need all of your Modern Meditation skills to nurture
it so it can grow. Awareness, too, isn't an intellectual exercise.
It has nothing to do with words, concepts or theories. It will
only grow when you stop thinking about Awareness.

AWARENESS EXPERIMENT

You can do this practical experiment with anything moving,
such as a river, the wind, or sunlight. You will find that you
enter the flow state we often talk about at **beanddo**, sometimes
referred to as 'rheosoma' or 'inscendence', which is the *process
of climbing into the world, into nature (inward and outward), into the
full human experience, wholehearted participation.*

1. *Go outside and find a comfortable and safe place to sit or stand.
   Take a few moments to reconnect to the mind-body practice until
   you feel you are as embodied as possible.*

2. *Then look – meditate with your eyes open. Direct your Attention
   and observe a tree, or trees, passing clouds, the moon or anything
   natural.*

3. *Remember, no words, labels or judgements. To start with, you
   are simply looking. If you need to, you can just repeat mentally,
   'looking... looking... looking...' Sure, your eyes are part of the
   process, but only partially as you are behind them. You are simply
   looking with your whole Conscious Awareness, receiving raw in-
   formation as it is now.*

4. *Notice when seeing kicks in. After a while, you might sense a deeper-flowing relationship. The distinction between you and what you are observing shifts. There will be a moment when you intermingle as you, as the observer and what you are observing collapses. You are connected as pure Awareness, fully alive to what is.*

So what are we saying here with this experiment – are trees, hills, and clouds conscious or aware? We can't really say. We know they emerge from the field of consciousness like everything else and are made of the flow we feel. Maybe the difference is a nervous system which allows us to be conscious of being conscious – *to be Aware of being Aware.*

That last part is key here. Cultivated Awareness will reveal more space, time, and insight as you observe and reflect the world from the inside out as you enjoy a shift that allows you to observe fully from a brand-new viewpoint. Being aware means having full agency over what you are doing and who you are, and what you are feeling. You have located and occupied, if only for a fleeting moment, a place from which you are fully alive and aligned with who you are and what you are doing.

Modern Meditation for
Cultivating Conscious Awareness

This next **A** practice– AWARENESS will merge with ATTENTION and allow you to build an inner expanding experience flowing along the vertical Being axis. You will start with your somatosensory ATTENTION practice, but after a while, awareness will unfold again all by itself. Remember you are setting the conditions for awareness to flow into your perception. It can't be forced. After a while, Awareness will feel like a spatially expanding dimension which seems to have nothing to do with who, where or what you are as a fixed individual physical body. You will notice your body and its surroundings fall into the background.

As you mix *Attention with Awareness,* you'll begin to switch on the focus of your meditation practice, the capacity to pay Attention to Attention and then ultimately being Aware of being Aware. This is the Awareness you want to uncover. A deep type of innate or natural Awareness is already present where you attend to Awareness itself as a thing in its own right rather than something inside your Awareness. After a while, the spatial expansion you feel as natural open awareness is the real you as a pure conscious sense of being. It will feel relaxed, effortless, empowering and expansive. With practice, this deep Awareness state will become very familiar and accessible in your day-to-day life when you apply the final two **A** practices, Attitude and Action.

Having cultivated your Attention skills, this expanded feeling of natural Awareness signifies you are getting close to the source of you. It brings an upgraded sense of connection, joy, compassion and creativity. You are YOU without prior conditions, agendas or expectations, ready to thrive.

MODERN MEDITATION FOR AWARENESS PRACTICE

1. *Begin your attention technique starting with your fingers and then toes as before. Remember, when you cultivate attention in the right way and then expand it onto more than one thing, Awareness will simply unfold and evolve.*

2. *There is a spatial quality to the experience. Awareness unfolds as a space, but you know it isn't empty – it's full of potential and possibility. Its qualities are love, peace, stillness, compassion, connection and creativity. Hold yourself there and place your Attention on Awareness. We can do this by following the flow of experience openly by staying with Awareness as it becomes aware, again like the Attention Practice, this is being Aware of being Aware.*

3. *As you sit, the experience will come from your body as a sensation. As each experience arises, simply mentally label it as 'sensation', or 'feeling', or even hearing'. Don't hang onto or try to resolve each experience as it rises and falls. It's not yours; it's simply arising from the nature of things happening all by themselves in the doing field.*

4. *You are only interested in the shift towards the centre, which comes from discovering how to be aware of the experience of the experience.*

Daily Conscious Awareness Strategies

The Awareness practice results in a pure and undifferentiated experience of simply being that underpins everything and everyone. If, after a while, you begin to feel a sense of connection, oneness and joy, then you will know why. Interestingly, we don't really have a word for this innate capacity. It's sometimes known as *isness, thusness, oneness* and so on... but don't stress about names here. You are moving beyond words.

1. There Is More
Start by feeling, seeing and hearing your way into a deeper perception of yourself and the world. There is more to you than you think or have been told. So know that you are building a new paradigm, a new, more authentic view of what is possible. Build Awareness, and don't let anyone or anything distract you.

2. Take Time to Check-in
Remind yourself often to find and occupy those still, quiet moments in the day to just stop and notice where you are, who you are with and what you are doing. You'll be surprised that your day is packed with opportunities to practice and feel aware.

3. Reflect on Everything
Your senses and nervous system are essentially a mirror reflecting innate Awareness of everything you do and say back to you. Use this to 'watch' yourself as you act in the world. This builds a positive reflective mindset that will help you create a little space between you and the world, operate from the inside out and stay centred and grounded at your node point.

4. Observe Everything

Be the observer of everything, including all feelings and emotions but not in a critical or judgemental way. Recognise when you are reacting using words to see and understand instead of actively observing to know and feel. Allow yourself to be fully present to others. Attend fully, and listen carefully without wanting to judge, intervene or manipulate.

5. Say What, Not Why

Awareness will evolve naturally once you pay Attention to the what rather than the why. Questions that most run through mentally like, why am I doing this? Why do I feel like this? Why does this person behave in a particular way? Searching for the why is pointless and will push you away from your node centre. Instead, go with what is happening without interference.

6. Keep a Notebook

As your awareness grows and your sensitivity develops, ideas, feelings and insight will come more and more to the front of your experience. Make sure you allow time to reflect on your moments of Conscious Awareness. You'll be surprised by what you will discover.

7. Stop Living in Your Head

You will become increasingly centred and grounded in reality as Awareness reveals a world of space, calm, opportunity and insight. More and more, you will notice that you forget where you are and start to inhabit the self–sabotaging world of fiction in your head. In other words, keep your thinking to a minimum. You will find Awareness will be more effective.

8. Trust Your Self

As your Awareness emerges, you will notice personal insights will evolve. New values will emerge, or existing ones will grow stronger. You might also find that values you previously thought were vital might just fall away. You will see, too, that you can trust yourself to do what is right and at the right time. You will know what to do and where to go as your deeper Awareness forms a guiding inner compass.

> You will know what to do and where to go as your deeper Awareness forms a guiding inner compass.

The Benefits of Conscious Awareness in Daily Life

- It engages insight and gives you the deep creative power to help shape and influence outcomes.

- It reveals how everything is just information flowing, happening according to their rules.

- It helps in knowing when things, thoughts, places, actions and people are not serving you.

- It helps you become a better decision-maker. It gives you more self-confidence – so, as a result, you can communicate with clarity and intention.

- It allows you to exist in a different temporal space where the stress of time pressure and imagined outcomes diminish.

- It will lead to more expansive and less reactive action helping to understand things from multiple perspectives as things just pass by.

- It helps you build better relationships.

- It allows you to regulate your emotions, keep a clear head and see the bigger picture.

- It decreases stress and makes you happier.

Affirmation

I remain engaged, attentive and centred on whatever events and experiences and actions flow through me.

Chapter 12

STRATEGIES FOR DEVELOPING A CONSCIOUS ATTITUDE

'Let your concern be with action alone, and never with the fruits of action. Do not let the results of action be your motive, and do not be attached to inaction'.

The Bhavagad Gita

So now your **Attention** is fine-tuned and directed with purpose along your perception continuum as your **Awareness of Awareness unfolds**.

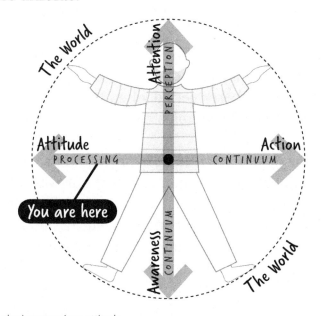

Figure 15: Developing conscious attitude.

The next Modern Meditation skill is **Attitude** as you move out into the world from the inside out onto the horizontal processing continuum. If the vertical axis, *Attention and Awareness*, is something you **are**, then *Attitude and Action* on the horizontal is something you **do**. Again it's all down to how you receive, process and experience daily in-formation. There is simple Modern Meditation Attitude Practice at the end of this section to help you do this.

Everything Happens

When discussing a different attitude, I'm talking about minimising or removing the **expectation we attach to action**. We expect certain things to happen. We want good things to happen and avoid bad things we don't want to happen. This mindset keeps us in a selfish, almost persistent state of stress and anxiety. Heightened expectation also attaches our attention to the future. We are no longer in the present as we try to look ahead and visualise what might or might not happen. Your brain is basically a prediction machine. We try to guess the outcome of our actions before they play out. This was fine during humanity's hunter gatherer period when life was simpler but less effective in our more complex age.

Well, here is the deal – everything happens, all of the time, whether you want them to or not. And there are outcomes, too, always. The world is in constant flux regardless of what you want. The world goes on in and of itself. It's all a process. That doesn't mean you are isolated. There are ways of fine-tuning and participating creatively, by adjusting and shifting your Attitude towards letting go, by doing through not doing. You don't need to try too hard on this. The shift in Attitude will happen as part of the Modern Meditation process. But it doesn't hurt to reflect on them now and see where your current Attitudes come from, how they make you feel and where they lead you.

We are taught from an early age that we are separate, individual and divided and, therefore, in opposition. In the west, we are mostly taught to *compare, compete and defeat*. We are told that we live in a fragmented world which needs constant control, interference and management. And that each of us is defined as a separate, isolated, competitive consumer caught up in a frantic, increasingly complex world. At the deepest level, most of us probably think, is this all wrong. But mistakenly, we continue to participate or have no choice, that to feel better, successful, or even survive, we must confront, struggle with, and insist that the world delivers what we expect from our life. In other words, we expect some reward, some return from our lives and the world.

'*Keep your eyes on the prize*' is the beloved catchphrase of many business and leadership strategists who demand that for anyone to be successful, a target or goal is required. Yes, it's great for a business to have a plan but do you personally need to have the same sort of strategic plan too?

It's really an invitation for disappointment at best, it's an illusion, and if your eyes are fixed there, your Attention is attached to an imaginary future event. You are not present while fixating on an imaginary life instead of the one you are actually living. That's where the real opportunity is.

I'm not dismissing success or achievement here. It's that real and lasting achievement that can only be created in the present. It's the only safe, nourishing and inspiring place where you are fully alive.

So your Attitudes towards external things are shaped over time, mostly by what you have been told. Attitudes are the result of judgements and expectations. We create them. Attitudes can come in all shapes and sizes, and they will if you let them interfere and totally dominate how you see and act. So there is only one Attitude you need to cultivate **non-attachment.**

Up until now, it's likely that your Attitude has been one of self-protection, want and desire, all focused on an imagined future or outcome. You might also feel you have all your personal Attitudes to the world and others set just right and that serve you in what you think you need. Really though? Like everything else, Attitudes and the mindsets that create them are not permanent, not fixed and not real. What if, instead, we shift our Attitude and reshape it to serve the moment's needs instead.

The new Attitude to cultivate is unconditional observation or choiceless Awareness. This means flowing with everything, absolutely without modification or restrictions.

Don't Interfere

You are now training your Attention and Awareness to be an *impartial observer* or *witness* of the flow of in-formation as it rises, passes and falls through your experience. This requires you to cultivate a new Attitude of non-interference, allowing everything to come no matter what. In a sense, you are learning to let go. Or better still, not **take on** or **interfere with the in-formation** that is flowing. This form of Attention then expands, becoming subtler as you learn to open up. Different mental attachments and judgments weaken, and your Attention gets deeper, softer and more expansive.

The new Attitude you are going to cultivate is *unconditional* observation or *choiceless* Awareness. This means flowing with everything, absolutely without modification or restrictions. In yoga, this Attitude of free perception is known as Aparigraha, often translated as 'non-greed' or 'non-possessiveness'. But it also points out something deeper in that our Attitude should focus on taking and responding to only what serves us and the world moment by moment.

Like the *Attention and Awareness, Attitude and Action* serve each other and can't be divided. This is the origin of that old cliche, *'It's the journey, not the destination.'* This is essentially saying that we should never concern ourselves with the outcome of a situation. We should only concern ourselves with what we're doing right now as we take action. I know this might seem hard. Don't worry; like everything we have talked about here, this new mindset will evolve naturally out of your practice.

What you are NOT going to do is to examine or judge or modify the experience of whatever you are directing your attention to. Neither will you claim any ownership or authorship of what is happening. You are simply going to observe so that your conscious sense of *Attention and Awareness* reveals a **conscious witness** to what is happening as it is happening. This will make you a creative node point for change in the world. But don't confuse yourself here. This doesn't mean giving up, being impassive, not caring or shutting down to what is happening or what you do. It's the opposite.

This might sound like a challenge – to let go like this, but you will soon realise it's a way of saying a big YES! in the form of an all-pervading acceptance to the flow – to what is happening no matter what. You will step away from resistance and go with it.

Not ME

Popular psychologists might call this flow or *Self-optimisation*. This is when you are ultimately connected to **your Self**, and it's a creative thing. I'm talking about creativity, not in terms of artistic ability. Instead, this is creativity in the shape of an intelligent force for change running through you right now.

To make this work, the primary **attitudinal** shift you need to cultivate is – **it's not all about you**. This is hard for most of us because we've been taught early on that it is all about '**you**'. If this is a surprise, you have much catching up to do. But it really isn't. It never has been.

In fact, the three words you should remove from your vocabulary as you work to upgrade your attitude through this process are I, Me and Mine. Those guys are trouble, so learn to recognise them and stay out of their way. If you don't know what I mean, look around you. There is bound to be someone in your workplace or community that acts selfishly, scheming, self-motivated by what they think they want or deserve and will do anything to achieve reward and status. Often manic identification with an ego like this has its roots in lack and emptiness, but that's another book.

Magical Reality

Developing unconditional, non-attached observation will sharpen and connect directly to your actual and real experience. It's switching on – a deep knowing and connection are engendered with whatever arises moment by moment. A profound singularity of place, moment, action and experience open up. There is a fleeting experience of *oneness*, an oceanic moment which delivers a deeper, more immediate magical reality of things known. A state of being in the world so often explored by artists.

Yes. I remember Adlestrop—
The name, because one afternoon
Of heat the express-train drew up there
Unwontedly. It was late June.

The steam hissed. Someone cleared his throat.
No one left and no one came
On the bare platform. What I saw
Was Adlestrop—only the name.

Adlestrop, Edward Thomas

Some artists have developed techniques that helped them
empower a non-attached Attitude. A sort of arm's length
approach which allowed them to see differences and create a
space of non-interference as the unfolding action of the work
happens. Matisse, for example, is famous for using a long
bamboo stick (about 2m in length) with charcoal fixed to the
end. This was designed to not only allow the artist to work at
scale but also build a spatial distance from the action where
the whole thing is seen at once. The Action was coupled with a
minimised control and execution of the line, which flowed by
its own rules, fuelled by Matisse's intention to act. In short,
Matisse was following the stick's movement and allowing the
action and the output to be shaped purely by process (in the
now) and not expectation of product (in the future).

I have utilised a non-attached mindset in my own work for many years. As an architect, I would often design in this way. Not using a long stick, but through my Modern Meditation practice, I became a vehicle for the pen and not the other way around. Now in my art making, I am exploring 'process or action painting'.

When your Attitude to work is used this way, you let go. To paraphrase Joseph Campbell, you let go of what you think you are planning to do, but instead, experience what is really there for you.

Figure 16: Night at the Bistro Californium (Pop – Bang – Whizz), Mick Timpson, 2022.

For me, painting is a vehicle for nurturing this new Attitude-based Action. It reveals how you can bring a whole new dimension to what you do, how you do it and how it makes you feel. Working this way is exciting, demanding, fulfilling and just about the most joyful thing you can do. But it does require a courageous letting go – another thing that comes with Modern Meditation practice. In the past, I would have relied on concepts or techniques that I had studied before or perhaps copied from someone else. If you are going to do that, focus on the motivation and insight of the artist rather than their product or output. Otherwise, what you do will feel unreal and most likely leave you feeling failure and pointlessness. This works not as **something to be** learned but as **a way to be**. Think about how you can apply this attitudinal shift to your actions.

MODERN MEDITATION FOR CONSCIOUS ATTITUDE

With your Attention and Awareness Practice, you are moving inwards. You can hopefully see that this inner shift is nothing to do with closing off the outside but reconnecting to it and seeing it all in high-definition. To maintain this new cognition, you must be vigilant about what the mind is doing. This is key.

1. *Return to your chair and log onto your somatosensory Attention Practice until you are flowing through your Awareness space.*

2. *The key here is remaining non-attached to what is happening. Your Attitude now must be this is all just happening. Every experience, including the body, sitting, breathing and sensing for you, is simply nature unfolding as it will.*

3. *You are, without an agenda, without wanting to judge or change anything. Your body-mind is relaxed, open, fully present and*

energised, ready to respond to new creative insights and ideas. This ongoing open Attitude isn't only vital in terms of maintaining and growing your sense of innate Awareness but also how it can be sustained as you go about your daily actions.

For example, as I type this sentence, I watch my fingers move across the keyboard. They know what to do. And it's the same with the words too. My Attitude is intention mixed with non-attachment as I witness every action and experience as something that arises out of the field, out of nature and the doing space. Meanwhile, I watch as it all flows. Many people report this experience as play. Just go with it.

If, however, my Attitude was one of ongoing critical analysis of what was happening, my enjoyment would fall, creativity would diminish, and ideas would be dead on arrival. This is the realm of your inner critic, who is also close friends with I, Me and Mine.

Daily Conscious Attitude strategy

With practice, you will discover that the knowing mind and not the judging or egocentric mind will take centre stage in your day-to-day life. From there, everything changes.

1. Not Knowing
Start by not having an agenda, not planning, not being driven by expectation and not being attached to the outcome. You don't own anything, most of all your work. And remember what Huxley told us at the beginning of this book – You are a conduit, not the source. Practise Modern Meditation to grow a space of insight to help you step back and out of your own way.

2. Keep Watching

Keep your attention directed with purpose. Maintain a deep engagement, slow down and take time to be present and aware. Practise Modern Meditation to see reality and know what's actually being asked for, moment by moment.

3. Don't Interfere

While you watch, accept what arises as in-formation, inside and out and go with it. Modern Meditation will help you stay out of any internal mental argument you might be having about what and why. Don't label, compare or categorise.

> Modern Meditation will help you
> stay out of any internal mental argument
> you might be having about what and why.
> Don't label, compare or categorise.

4. Follow the Energy

Learn how to follow the paths and opportunities that arise for you. New directions are always opening up as you live and work every moment of possibility. You will know when they happen and where they are because they flow with potential creative energy. Your Modern Meditation practice will help you distinguish between what you think you should be doing and knowing what you are doing.

5. Don't Own It

It's not about you and your notions of success or failure. It's great to be good at what you do and accept any reward but never assume it's yours. As soon as you align what you do with personal ownership and value, it will bring you a life of disappointment and fear. Use Modern Meditation to help you develop a space between you and the world.

6. Don't Interpret

Notice too, when your mind starts a narrative about you and your relationship to what is happening. This is good, this is bad etc. Use your Modern Meditation skill to see the difference between the ego-fuelled interpretation of what you think is right and insight that tells you what is right.

7. Know How to Start and Stop

This last Attitude takes us back to the beginning. Approaching everything you do with *'What's in it for me'* Attitude, or *'I might fail'*, *'I don't trust myself to do this'*, or *'How will people judge me and what I'm doing'*, *'This isn't good enough'* will compress and kill the flow of possibilities. Use your Modern Meditation practice to manage that *inner critic* and trust yourself you are good enough to know what needs to be done and what doesn't.

Benefits of a Conscious Attitude

The seven attitudinal shifts I have outlined above are probably the most important things you can learn. They can't be forced, though. To grow these shifts naturally and effortlessly, they must be cultivated with regular Modern Meditation.

There's a lot to be gained by practising non-attachment and adding it as a life skill. Benefits of non-attachment include a clearer mind, a better mood, more mental space for the things you can control (as opposed to the things you can't), and less fear regarding change. In relationships, it can also help you to avoid unhealthy or toxic co-dependent situations.

Affirmation

It's impossible to feel empty, useless and lost. Being conscious in Attitude means being whole, purposeful and effective.

Chapter 13

STRATEGIES FOR DEVELOPING CONSCIOUS ACTION

'We were made for joy and woe,
And when this we rightly know,
Through the world we safely go.'

William Blake

We are now at the other end of the horizontal processing continuum. This final orientation is about ACTION. Now you come to the shift that makes real-time changes in life by making everything you do an open, unconditioned conscious experience – a meditation.

Figure 17: Developing conscious action.

Action Is All in the Now

In exploring Attitude, in Chapter 12, we saw how loosening the self-made tethers of Attachment to wants, outcomes, rewards, or ownership increased our connection to everything. This *non-attached* observation or choiceless, unconditional Awareness allows us to perceive and experience, with high-definition, all in-formation that arises.

Now we add this new insight to Action. Not in terms of **what** Action you take but **how** the Action is undertaken. That's the key! It's here that you experience your new **Conscious Attitude** not only as an observer of this purposeful, intelligent flow happening right now but also as a *creative collaborator*.

So we conclude this final **A** practice knowing that all life is Action, happening right now. How you perceive and process, Action opens up a whole new world. Action is internal and external, finite on the surface, and infinite internally. You need to pay close Attention to even the most mundane, hitherto unconscious Action. You need to feel it flow as Awareness and shape it through Attitude because, at its core, there is a seed of creation and, therefore, a means of transformation. And because, as the teachers and artists tell us, true creation is joy, it's not to be missed.

If this sounds too esoteric, try the practice and find out for yourself.

It's here in Action where you'll begin to see and understand your relationship to your mind and body and how, ultimately, they are designed to work together and operate for the welfare of others and the world. Action now is seen as one of Attitude and ultimately then of purpose. It's about seeing Action, not in terms of outcome and wants but primarily of purpose. And what is that purpose? *Keeping the world going* because it's worth it. Don't get confused here. When I talk of purpose, I am not channelling a business coach, nor am I talking about ambition, which is striving to reach a certain goal in the future. Remember, only Now is real, and only in the moment can you make any difference for yourself and the world. Your purpose in Action will reveal itself once you find that node space of oneness. You might be surprised by what you discover.

If the first three practices, Attention, Awareness and Attitude, reveal this new and different relationship, then it's in Action that we bring what we have realised and discovered back into the world. And what characterises this *Conscious Action?* **Everything you do will have a flowing, effortless rightness to it**. It will feel like you are doing nothing because it will feel obvious, right and effortless. It stands to reason that if your Action is aligned with the nature of the universe, it is purposeful and necessary. At the cosmic level, nothing is unnecessary or overdone. This is Conscious Action in Action.

'You should also remember to ask yourself on every occasion, "Is this something that is really necessary?"'

Marcus Aurelius [18]

---

18. Marcus Aurelius. Meditations. Book 4, translated by Robin Hard. (Oxford World Classics 2011); 28-29

It is not, however, staying in bed and doing nothing! The key here isn't *what* Action you take but **how you see** the Action happening. Don't think you can do anything you want if you make it a meditation. That's ego kicking in, and you'll soon find it doesn't work that way, leaving you back where you started. You are responsible.

Similarly, don't pick apart your Actions. Sitting and analysing your Actions while undertaking them will create hesitation and procrastination, the two things you need to avoid if you want to get out of your light. Conscious Action requires trust, energy and courage, which you will nurture in abundance in your formal Modern Meditation practice. And don't worry because Conscious Action will always present you with the right choices and solutions.

When you rotate back into your fully conscious node point, your true Self, and engage with Action from there, you will see that whatever you do, you get it right the first time. You won't get entangled in the distracting and stress-inducing, non-essential stuff and most likely fail.

Instead, follow the process unfolding in the field. Do what's right in front of you, consciously, without judging. If you want to make all Actions conscious, you need to change how you perceive the Action as it's being performed by your mind-body in real-time. All Action happens in the present. However, we are so close to this activity emerging in the present that it simply goes unnoticed. We can miss so much of our lives.

Action, then in its purest form, is like everything else, flowing in-formation, a field of real-time raw data. You are constantly in *receive* and *transmit* mode, adapting to this in-formation as it flows and interacts, creating never-ending chains of cause and effect beyond your current context of time and space, but always in the now.

> All Action happens in the present. However, we are so close to this activity emerging in the present that it simply goes unnoticed. We can miss so much of our lives.

Creating that space by making the unconscious conscious will change how you operate in the world and how in turn, the world operates. It's a profound, creative thing. You'll know it when it happens. No doubt you have heard of the yogic concept of *karma*. Most people use it incorrectly. Karma actually means work or Action. Its Sanskrit root is *'Kri'*, which we find in English as *'create', 'creation' and 'creativity'*. This is a vital insight.

'Every little work in life, however humble, can become an act of creation and therefore a means of salvation, because in all true creation we reconcile the finite [doing] with the Infinite [being], hence the joy of creation. When vision is pure and when creation is pure there is always joy.'

The Bhagavad Gita [Introduction] (Penguin Classics).
Trans. Juan Mascaro 1960

I often read the above quote in my yoga classes because it captures the whole **beanddo** concept of Conscious Action. The point here is that at the heart of every little Action– walking the dog, sitting in meetings, at the supermarket, are acts of creativity; it's just that most of the time, we are never in the right mindset to notice. But when we do, it all feels joyful – a true act of creativity and liberation right in the heart of the every day – exposing the infinite inside the finite, as William Blake invited us to see *'a world in a grain of sand'*.

Stop and reflect on this for a moment. You might be thinking, but I hate walking the dog, doing the shopping, and going to meetings! That's I, Me and Mine interfering again. But despite this, I can guarantee that you have experienced (probably quite often) a sudden, momentary fusion of joy with Action and purpose that seems to rise out of nowhere with nothing to do with where you are and what you're doing. We often ignore or don't choose this shift because we have never developed the tools. Imagine, though, being able to switch on this deeper connection wherever you are and whatever you are doing? It's possible with your Modern Meditation practice. So the individual who acts consciously, nurtured by bringing the right *Attention, Awareness and Attitude to all Action*, becomes both a creator and an act of creation. One can become a portal of creative change; they are inspired and inspire others.

> The point here is that at the heart of every little Action- walking the dog, sitting in meetings, at the supermarket, are acts of creativity; it's just that most of the time, we are never in the right mindset to notice.

The most fundamental and creative Action we experience moment by moment is breathing. In fact, the word *inspiration* is connected to the Latin *inspiratus,* meaning 'to breathe into, inspire' and since the 16th century, has meant 'the drawing of air into the lungs'. This breathing sense is still commonly used among medics, as is expiration ('the act or process of releasing air from the lungs'). However, before inspiration was used to refer to breath, it had a distinctly esoteric meaning in English, referring to a divine influence, to be *inspired* by something divine.

Ask yourself why you are breathing, where does breathing come from, and who exactly is doing the breathing? It's not you, is it? You can interfere with it and shape it into conscious breathing, a cornerstone of yoga practice, but it works happily on its own.

This is why most artists and creatives who have worked out how to make a living connecting to their inner selves, that deeper intelligence, are sometimes initially stumped when asked what their inspiration was for an idea – they don't know. It happens mostly all by itself, the artist is the vehicle, and it's liberating. The artist John Hoyland, after a lifetime of painting, concluded that he had got to a point where he liked to: '... *try and make these pictures paint themselves. The less you impose, the fresher it is. Painting is a kind of alchemy.*' [19]

This is then *Conscious Action*. Not so much taking Action as letting the Action happen by being a portal and instrument of change and collaborating with its flow. It puts us in touch with

---

19. *Interview with critic Andrew Lambirth in 2008 interview.*
http://www.johnhoyland.com/paintingsother-work/

something fundamental. As Frank Lloyd Wright said, stay close to it.

'An idea is salvation by imagination. Study nature, love nature, stay close to nature. It will never fail you.'

Frank Lloyd Wright

Where Does Action Come From?

Now we go back to where we started with David Bohm's quantum insight: 'Consciousness is never static or complete but is an unending process of movement and unfoldment.' You and I exist in and are simultaneously formed by a unified flowing field of wholeness. This field is Consciousness and it's the ground from which everything emerges.

In an interview with his friend William M. Angelo's [20] two years before his passing, Bohm described an experience in his early childhood. He was with friends in the mountains, crossing a rapidly flowing stream filled with rocks, and describes feeling 'very apprehensive; it was a new situation.' However, he realised to cross, he had to jump from one rock to the next without stopping rather than step by step. He describes how the experience made a deep impression on his work in consciousness: He said, 'Consciousness is going, moment by moment of awareness... and not mapped out.'

20. *'A Conversation with Professor David Bohm', The Bohm–Krishnamurti Project; https://bohmkrishnamurti.com/beyondlimits/*

Not mapped out! What a wonderful phrase. Sure it's important to plan for things like holidays, designing bridges, and visiting the dentist. But each event isn't planned in the now, but when they happen, they are the now. If we think we can map out everything, we are just interfering with the process, allowing I, Me and Mine to filter out the world and all its possibilities. You, too, may have very similar experiences where you have not mapped out what might happen in favour of an overall Awareness in which the right thing effortlessly happened, directly responsive to the needs of the moment, no matter what.

What Bohm is talking about here is a *flow* experience which we all have from time to time, mostly accidentally, and when circumstances dictate that you don't think, you just do. How often have you overthought something leading to you falling off that bike, spoiling that artwork, dropping that ball, or overworking that report?

So your life's Action is continually folding and unfolding, defined only by the present context flowing in your Doing field. It's a never-ending process of change that many are hardly aware of. We see this continuing process happening all around us. It's the principle of cause and effect, and it's the force that drives nature, you and me.

You might think that you have total control, and that it's all down to you. That's an illusion projected onto I, Me and Mine in tandem with the modern world. Remember that scene in Walt Disney's Pinocchio (which traumatised many of my generation back in the day) when Pinocchio was dancing on the stage with other puppets, singing, *'I have no strings on me'*? He got so carried away with his own sense of destiny, uniqueness and ego that he soon slipped up and fell into all the other stringed puppets and became completely entangled, bringing the dance to an abrupt end.

'It is as if dancing puppets imagine they are the dancers rather than merely puppets, and because of this illusion they become increasingly entangled in the strings.'

The Bhagavad Gita

We are all dancing, but in many ways, you aren't doing anything at all. It's your mind-body that is doing all the work. But what we do is interfere with it constantly, assuming we need to take charge and map things out. But once you stop interfering with the Action using Modern Meditation techniques, you realise you are a vital conduit, a focus point, a node for continuous Action in the world. You then start seeing the process, and you begin to participate, collaborate, and shape it.

Knowing that it's all happening according to its own rules, you might feel what's the point if it appears I can't make a difference and gain some control? Well, that's not true. The irony is that once you learn to let go, you gain control and start living, creating a self-world based on an inner sense of meaningful connection, expanded Awareness, creativity, equanimity, and contentment. All you need is to get with the programme. To be Aware of being Aware. It's what the universe has been waiting for all this time.

As Action is a constant, Conscious Action is simply paying close unconditional observation to all thoughts, feelings, ideas, sensations and activity using your new Modern Meditation skills. This means working differently with *all 10 of your senses.* Remember, your senses are transceivers here. They are the interface between the outer and inner worlds. They work all by themselves.

Imagine that you, as your mind-body, is like a building with 10 openings. What the openings have in common is that they are all doors. Five are entrance doors, and five are exit doors. The entrance doors are your senses through which raw in-formation comes and goes. If we can, as William Blake defines, manage to keep these doors of perception held open, unobstructed or unlocked, these openings link our inner world to our outer world, unifying Being and Doing.

Meditation really does open doors. These five entrance doors are your passive, automatic cognitive senses that *import* information from the world around you, leading directly to your perception continuum. These are touch, hearing, smell, taste and vision. Five exit doors are connected to the processing continuum and *export* in-formation expressed as you in Action back into the world. These include eliminating waste products such as the excretion of urine and carbon dioxide, reproduction, talking, moving and grasping. You are the resident of this building. You as pure Self, looking out onto the world. These mind-body *filters* or *portals* of action collect in-formation from the doing field inside and outside of you as they simply roll on daily. It's fundamentally nature at work, and you and I are intrinsically part of it. Drawing attention to these doors, being aware of how they work, getting in behind them and then keeping them open with the right attitude, not interfering with what or who comes and goes across each threshold is the core of Modern Meditation. When outside and inside finally link together. You are unified and whole.

'We are internally related to everything, not [just] externally related. Consciousness is an internal relationship to the whole, we take in the whole, and we act toward the whole.'

David Bohm

By observing these 10 doors in daily life through modern meditation, you naturally move inwards, becoming increasingly aware of that inner conscious observing Self. You see more clearly how you, as the Self as consciousness, are independent of actions, senses and thoughts, sensations and wants. It doesn't mean not enjoying life and its actions and sensory experiences. Rather, these are enjoyed more fully, in a spirit of wisdom, freedom, and non-attachment. It can be energising, and it's happening right now, everywhere. Even when running a marathon, you can do the same thing.

When I ran the Manchester Marathon, I wanted to **bring my full attention to what I was doing rather than being distracted by thinking.** That meant no headphones, although I wasn't ready to release my running watch. I knew I would be distracted by tracking my pace. I know running with my tracking watch challenges me to run faster, but this is also ego-driven. My attitude towards running at a consistently strong pace, so I achieve my personal best. Essentially so I can then share this new personal best with anyone who will listen so they know that not only I can do a marathon, but I can do it fast too. Admittedly for the first 13 miles, I was running at a strong 9-minute mile pace and running with the 4-hour pacer. If you haven't run a race, this is someone who has a big flag on their backpack suggesting if you stay with them, you will do the race in the specified time. After keeping this up for miles, I let the 4-hour pacer person go. I knew my attention was on not losing the 4-hour pacer. And I was missing out on everything else. You could say I chose joy over speed.

In meditation practice, we bring Attention to the Action and not our expectations. Expectation takes you out of the present moment. Instead, we practice simply observing what is really happening. Quieting our minds from describing or analysing everything. If you're new to meditation, this may sound tricky, but it's all just practice – and some days, you will find it easier than others. We're humans – we ebb, and we flow! When I removed the expectation of running at a faster pace, I focused on the action. I observed my body running. I experienced the feelings and sensations in my body. This was indeed a sensation of burning in the legs and bum area. I noticed as my body was running for me it just knew what to do. **And when we notice our body in action, we are coming into the present moment.** Our body is always in the present moment, not like our mind when often our attention is elsewhere. This technique we use in meditation; we can practise noticing our fingers and toes and expanding our attention to our whole body. How often do you walk down the road and don't remember the walk because you were lost in thoughts of the mind? By bringing attention to the body and the present moment, **we can shift from unconscious reaction to Conscious Action.** Opening up to the full experience doesn't mean grasping at the positive and resisting the negative experience. It means accepting fully what is. I found the run very emotional. The support from the supporters and from the other runners. People running for Ukraine, and people running for loved ones. A quote from the movie Love Actually is 'love really is all around' and as we say at beanddo, 'the world is made up of love'. I really felt the love. I felt all the emotions. And all the burning pain in my legs and glutes. Instead of feeling like the run came and went in a fog, I remember it with a lot of clarity. I really felt awake. Like I really soaked up the experience.

Becs Mansfield, Beanddo trained Modern Meditation Teacher

It is liberating to accept everything as it is. We understand that to thrive, we can't choose Action. **If we stay present and make the right intention, the right Action and output choose us.** And if we avoid Action, procrastinate and instead listen to that inner critic, we resist not only being ourselves but also our true purpose. You have got to keep engaged and aware.

Everything you need is right in front of you.

PART THREE

How Do We Make Action Conscious?

When you observe and see the action, a new space of Awareness
opens up between you and what you are doing. This space
isn't a division or barrier, nor does it obscure, as a sense
of full immersion, connection and engagement unfold. You
will notice that the experience of the Action intensifies.
Everything becomes more immediate, flowing with continuity
and rightness, where Conscious Action becomes right Action.
Senses sharpen, and every movement seems to be happening
all by itself but in a way that supports and gives meaning to the
moment. This Awareness space also allows one to expand time
and space and see Action unconditionally as it rises and falls
in all its parts, no matter how fast or automatic. We see three
components to any Action (as long we don't interfere mentally).
There is a doer, the doing and the thing being done. In other
words, the ever-changing conditions of the doing field or Nature
as the maker, the means of making and the thing being made.
Try this little exercise. You are going to observe the mechanics
of action. As you sit and read this book, you will split the Action
into three parts – the doer, the doing and the thing being done.

The Doer: This is you in terms of mind and body in Action in
real time. Become aware of the whole thing in Action. As you
begin to observe that shift of perception, that indicates it's not
me that is sitting and reading; *it's the mind-body. It knows what to
do without me interfering.*

The Doing: This is the Action taking place in real time. It's arising as pure in-formation out of the ground of consciousness. Fuse with it directly. Observe your mind-body as it sits and holds the book. Observe as you watch your eyes focus and move across the page. Observe how your senses are taking in the information and your mind as it processes the information into an understanding or insight. Doing it is all about the process. Watch and observe the process without interfering.

The thing being done: Don't see yourself as the source of Action by owning, judging or analysing. The doing is rising and falling, appearing and disappearing in constant change. Again this has nothing to do with you, the real you. It's just happening as part of nature. Just observe, merge with it and see, if only for a moment, that deeper reality that lies under the everyday Action of sitting and reading.

MODERN MEDITATION FOR CONSCIOUS ACTION

Don't try too hard on this practice. You can start by dividing the moment into three, but it will soon become one conscious event. Observe without interference as you move around the world. Getting up in the morning, standing, walking, eating, bathing, doing anything. Use your Modern Meditation skills to constantly concentrate your *Attention, Awareness and Attitude on the Action*, the doing of it and not on your assumed relation to the act or its character or value.

1. *Return to your seat and set up your mind–body as before by relaxing and feeling your body in the chair.*

2. *Be aware of your intention to sit the body. Be aware of its shape and posture as it sits for you. Place your hands in your lap with palms upwards.*

3. *Take a moment to reflect on the three aspects of what you are doing – the doer, the doing and the thing being done.*

Maintain this practice, and your mind–body should become like a mirror reflecting things without judging or retaining them. You simply perceive without thoughts or analysis as everything around you, and in you, simply rise and fall as continuous flowing wholeness. There is walking, there is standing, there is talking, there is thinking, there is holding. There is no 'I am walking, I am doing this, it is a good thing, it is disagreeable, I am gaining merit, it is I who is realising how wonderful it is. We saw earlier in Conscious Attitude how these mindsets cause failure and unhappiness.

So instead of all this, simply practice Modern Meditation based perception of the mind-body on the act itself so that every Action becomes conscious. Making your day a continuous meditation will gradually develop mental clarity, becoming a more effective conduit for insight, creativity, peace and joy. Keeping with day-to-day application combined with formal practice and after a while, you will notice that your inner core and source of you, your-Self finds expression in the world. From here, fears of failure begin to melt away in favour of a joyous never-ending flow.

Daily Conscious Action Strategies

1. Try Not to Map Things Out (Too Much)

Having a goal is fine but don't start by over planning or trying to map out what will or might happen later before you even start. Already you are holding yourself hostage and diminishing your ability to be conscious and act from a deeper place. The solution will come when you use your Modern Meditation skills to shift you into a different mindset. It's good to have a goal but keep them at a distance. Stay focused and present, minimise expectation and the outcome will surprise you.

2. Stop Thinking!

Thought is psychological time as each thought you have is either made of the past or the future, dragging you out of the reality of the current action. Use your Modern Meditation skills to manage any mental narrative and hold you present and fully immersed in what you are doing, so that critical thoughts about what is happening cannot take hold. It's at this point your inner wisdom and creativity takes over.

3. Don't Be Afraid to Do Things Differently
Sure there are tried and tested ways to do things but they mostly become habitual and not always beneficial. Take risks in how you approach things. It's okay to be unsure, thoughtfully thoughtless and open to new suggestions and ideas. It takes courage to say – 'I don't know yet', but that is the skill here. You do know what to do but you have to let go and take Conscious Action to make it happen.

4. Stay focused and Be Quiet
Cultivating Conscious Action is making everything you do a meditation so context is important. Avoid distraction and choose environments that don't overwhelm or compete for your Attention.

5. Accept the Challenge
Things only look difficult or unachievable because you think they are. Know too that nothing is fixed, certain or permanent. Action is inevitable and everything changes, including you. This will help you understand that complexity, setbacks and obstacles are also part of the deal. Practice Modern Meditation to nurture a flow of non-resistance which will help you empower and transform the process where needed.

6. Be Fearless
The more you use your Modern Meditation skills the more you will feel resilient, purposeful and clear in what you do. Notice when I, Me and Mine, your own inner critics want to get involved and undermine you. Learn from others but don't copy them and trust you already have the tools to do what you are for. Remember, on a global scale the problems of the world

originate inside not outside. Change your inside and the outside changes.

7. Keep Watching

And finally, it's all about perception. Stay at your node point, watch yourself in action all the time. Notice often when you perceive any interference or incoherence that dislodges you away from your centre. Remember it's not **you** taking Action – it's your body-mind.

Benefits of Conscious Action in Daily Life

Perhaps then, *Conscious Action* is the application of wisdom sourced from an internal intuitive knowing. Finding the source of the real Action here will ensure you know how to use it. It will tell you what should be done and what shouldn't, what fear and courage are. It will help you know what bondage and resistance are and what freedom is. That is how wisdom works, and you will feel it. You will know it, and the more you stay centred and focused, the more you cultivate being in the centre, and the more you will recognise how your innate wisdom propels and guides you through inspired action.

Everything Is New

So here is the deal. When you learn to navigate to your central node and operate and observe Action from there, you notice a distinction between your Being and Doing. A space opens and links to the source, so when you act, you are operating from the point of genuine authenticity. Acting this way taps into deep wisdom, returning you to a knowing consciousness, the ground from which everything grows.

> It's the action the universe wants you to take. Welcome back to operating in line with your dharma.

I have said this before, but this happens when the thinking stops regarding expectation. Instead, you link with deep knowledge and intention and operate at a higher level where everything feels new and full of possibility. Creativity is something you have an inexhaustible supply of. Like love, the more you use it, the more you have. The courage this takes will come to you as you develop your practice. This attitude of a *beginner's mind* might give you the sweats to begin with, but it will always work and eventually liberate you:

'For me, every day is a new thing. I approach each project with a new insecurity, almost like the first project I ever did... I'm not sure where I'm going. If I knew where I was going, I wouldn't do it.'

Frank Gehry

When you take Action from the point of wisdom, you will notice everything happens easily. There is a flowing effortlessness to your body as it carries out actions. Action carried out this way is in harmony not only with yourself but with others too. It's the action the universe wants you to take. Welcome back to operating in line with your dharma. If you decide to take Action differently, say Action inspired and shaped by selfish desires, from negative habits, you will know that too because it will come with a distinct inner feeling, a pain, a doubt, an emotion that rises to say this isn't right. This is going against what is needed at that moment. You will feel it when it happens. Inner peace is lost. Sense of harmony and balance is lost.

Affirmation

I know what to do at any given moment. For me, there is always a solution.

PART THREE

PART FOUR
MODERN MEDITATION: BRINGING IT ALL TOGETHER

'Meditation... twice a day, every day. It has given me effortless access to unlimited reserves of energy, creativity and happiness deep within. This level of life is sometimes called "pure consciousness"—it is a treasury. And this level of life is deep within us all.'

~ *David Lynch*

Chapter 14

CREATING A WHOLE NEW WORLD

'We are internally related to everything, not [just] externally related. Consciousness is an internal relationship to the whole, we take in the whole, and we act toward the whole. Whatever we have taken in determines basically what we are.'

David Bohm

Hopefully, you have some insight into the opportunities and skills you have to change your world from the inside out and what it might feel like once you get the practice working. Now it's time to start designing and drawing out your new YOU. Don't worry, it's very simple. Practice is the key. Let the four new **A** skills develop together, like fingers on a hand. Through practice, we begin to see there are two aspects to Modern Meditation: formal and informal. Your formal practice is a regular sitting Modern Meditation practice. Your informal practice is applying the same skills to your everyday world and activity so that everything you do is a meditation. So far, I have explained the four skills as separate practices. Now you need them to become one. This will take time, but it's worth sticking with and exploring to keep your Attention towards the project and process of being You.

Your formal practice is a regular sitting Modern Meditation practice. Your informal practice is applying the same skills to your everyday world and activity so that everything you do is a meditation.

Finding the Right Wave

This in-formation that's coming to you from all directions in your field of doing is like a carrier wave containing more information than you might imagine, need or immediately understand. There is potential inside the in-formation wave wanting to be expressed and consciously realised by you. So how do you know when you have faithfully and consciously translated that wave into where you are and what you're doing? *You feel it.*

An effective way of thinking about this is *seeing* everything that happens, including all thoughts, feeling, and actions as waves on the ocean surface constantly rising and falling – this is your Doing. The ocean they rise from is your Being.

'When one's actions are not based on desire for personal reward, one can easily steady the mind and direct it towards the Atma, the True Self Within.'

The Bhagavad Gita

The point of all Modern Meditation based practices is to apply them to your everyday life. The real challenge and best outcome are to practice in the noise and distractions of work, home or wherever. Aldous Huxley defined this aspect of meditation practice in terms of being a research scientist. Formal daily practice can be described as laboratory work, working, experimenting and exploring in controlled conditions, or sitting on your chair in your chosen meditation space. The real benefits come through 'field work' where the same techniques and insights are tested and used in the unpredictable rough and tumble of the everyday, external world.

Preparing for Formal Practice

First, posture is important because Modern Meditation is a whole body-mind practice. This doesn't mean your practice won't be successful if you can't manage or maintain posture. What is really required is the increasingly effective skill of turning your Attention around 180 degrees inwards and becoming embodied as much as possible.

You can sit cross-legged on a cushion if you like, but most will find the posture challenging, particularly if they have not practised any physical yoga, which strengthens the spine and opens up the hips and knees etc. Instead, use a simple upright chair with a straight back and no armrests.

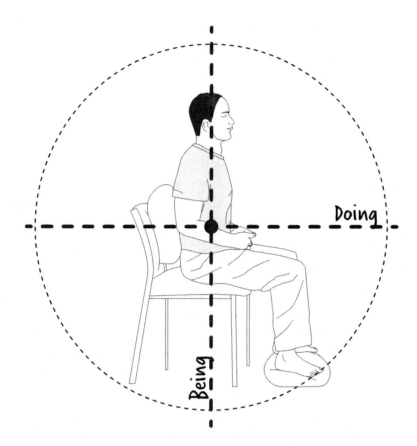

- Upper back positioned away from the chair support
- Spine lifted and straight
- Shoulders relaxed and dropping back
- Head held still
- Simple chair with no armrests
- Support lower back into angle of chair or use a small cushion
- Eyes closed or partially open
- Softly tuck chin
- Lift and open chest
- Breathe naturally through the nose. Close the mouth and allow the tongue to rest in the roof of the mouth
- Hands open and resting upwards on lap
- Legs parallel and knees pointing forward
- Feet flat on the floor (no shoes) Rest on cushion if feet can't reach the floor comfortably

Figure 18: Preparing for Modern Meditation practice.

As you develop your formal practice (twice a day if possible), you will likely notice and be surprised by mental and emotional obstacles, barriers and filters that look insurmountable and unavoidable.

Don't worry here. Remember, earlier, we talked about mental and emotional habits that you can get stuck in. Now, you are noticing, probably for the first time, the stuff that has been holding you back, obscuring reality and making you feel tired and frustrated as you try and make sense of it. Seeing these objects is a sign you are making great progress (it might also come with an initial feeling of liberation that will inspire you to keep going) and reveals that unconscious habits and reactions emerging out of your lower mind, your Default Mode, are now being revealed and observed (not resisted though). It's the noticing that is key. You are not invited to change or tackle anything. Use your new perceiving and processing insights described earlier. Observe, and they will naturally fall away. You don't break them down with effort, analysis or force. Nor do you try and 'change' with those enforced mindsets and corporate growth techniques sold at huge costs by so-called get rich and successful instantly self-empowerment business programmes.

You simply sit and watch.

Common Obstacles

There are four common obstacles that you might experience when you start practising:

1. Sinking

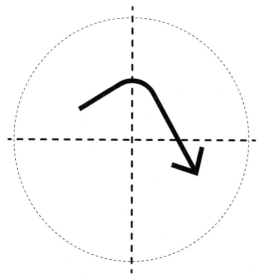

Figure 19: Avoiding obstacles to your practice – sinking.

Sometimes you will notice that you begin to sink or slouch. You might begin to feel sleepy or simply not very embodied or connected. Your Attention here isn't so much distracted as *switched off*. Your Awareness fades and is replaced with a sleepy dullness. Don't worry. The key is to notice this and return to a more conscious posture. Just lift yourself up and softly switch on your Attention again. You will also notice that the shape of your posture and breathing is also linked to what your mind is doing (and vice versa). If you drop back into your unconscious Default Mode, your body will tense or slump accordingly.

2. Drifting

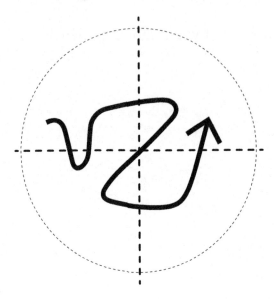

Figure 20: Avoiding obstacles to your practice – drifting.

This is when your Attention becomes distorted or involved with something other than where you need it. Before you know it, you will find that your Attention is locked into a continuous, ruminating mental narrative, which causes you to drift away from what you are doing and where you are. You will often find yourself not present at all. Noticing this and bringing yourself back is part of the practice. Don't ever feel that drifting off means you can't meditate. You can. Noticing that your Attention has drifted away from the Now is a key meditation skill. Even the most experienced meditators will constantly pull away from a mindless drifting. It's better to be *thoughtfully thoughtless than thoughtlessly thoughtful.*

3. Struggling

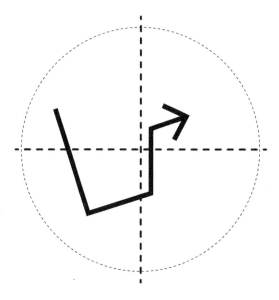

Figure 21: Avoiding obstacles to your practice – struggling.

If you are feeling, it's too hard for you, that is because you are trying *too hard*. The trick with meditation is to catch it and not force it or expect anything new to happen. Meditation isn't a destination. It's a state of being and experience that isn't related to something you 'do'; it's something you already are. Effortless effort is required. Learning not to try too hard for many of us feels counterintuitive. You might think that surely this magnitude of inner change described here requires a huge commitment of time and energy. Commitment, yes, but you will be surprised that you have all the time and energy you need. It will increase without going to the gym, as you discover how to just sit, Be and Do.

4. Attaching

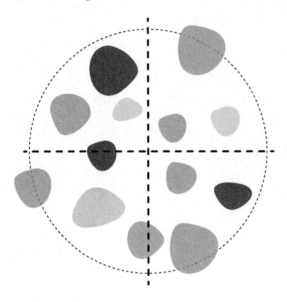

Figure 22: Avoiding obstacles to your practice – attaching.

All of the obstacles described here are very likely happening
because you are attaching to a particular outcome. Remember
the *non-attached attitude* we explored in your processing
continuum. Don't attach or claim anything as yours, such as my
feelings, thoughts, sensations, my frustration, my anxiety etc.
None of these belongs to you. If you start attaching to thoughts,
you will ruminate and follow a story until your meditation
becomes clouded. Remember thoughts think themselves. They
are simply passing in-formation made of objects that rise,
combine, tangle, untangle and fall. Never feel that it won't work
for you. It will. Meditation is a process, not a destination. All
you need to do is practice, and before you realise you will get it.

The Practice

Remember your body and all its raw experience, as in-formation flowing inside your sensory space, is already in the present moment. So before you start, just remind yourself you are already there. All you need to do now is occupy and inhabit that space fully. You go through yourself to your Self.

This is the challenge. At one level, it's therapeutic. On another, it's life changing.

Start by setting your coordinates. Breathe out, switch on and affirm to yourself the four skills:

Attention − Falls into the NOW. I am going inwards.

Awareness − I begin to expand as a space of pure experience.

Attitude − There are no expectations, no demands, just pure being.

Action − Is constant rising and falling within, around but without me.

Below is the Modern Meditation practice. Of course, once you sit and prepare for practice and lower your eyes, it will be impossible to follow. I suggest you read it through first.

Modern Meditation Practice

Carefully, follow the process and after a while, with practice, you will realise that all new experiences that begin to unfold for you will stick with you. Your nervous system and neural networks will remember the deeper experience and rewire accordingly.

*We will start on your vertical Being axis. Attention and Awareness is how you modify and enhance your perception. Maintain that space, and then connect to your horizontal **Attitude–Action Doing** axis. When the two lines cross, you are there... **your job is to stay there...***

1. *Return to your meditation spot and get comfortable. Drop your feet flat onto the floor, feet pointing forward, allowing them to root down.*

2. *Your hands are resting on the lap, with your palms facing upwards.*

3. *When you are ready, gently close or lower your eyes. Shoulders relaxed, feet relaxed and breathing normally through the nose.*

4. *Take a moment to find your posture. Adopt an alert but gentle position, sitting upright and coming into your space.*

5. *Sit away from the backrest and feel that slight lifting of the spine and the chest.*

6. *Try visualising the chair coming up to support you as you fall into your space. Become aware of the body being still, upright and supported in space.*

Intention Setting

And remember now that the purpose of this little gentle practice is to help you stop and change perspective and move inwards towards your centre. Affirm your intention to just be...

- *I am exactly where I planned to be.*

- *I am doing exactly what I planned to do.*

- *There is nowhere else to be. There is nothing else to do. This is it. Only now is it real.*

Attention

1. *Direct your attention to your fingers.*

2. *See if you can feel the fingertips as they radiate in response to your Attention. No need to move them, no need to look at them. Just be there. Almost immediately, you will feel a small but very noticeable sensation, a tingling, a gentle radiant sensation.*

3. *You want to sustain this sensation. Keep that somatic response to your Attention. It is held in place by your directed Attention as you sustain that buzzing feeling. So already, you are falling into the present. You can feel it. You are present.*

4. *Now while maintaining Your Attention on your hands, extend your attention down to the toes and the feet.*

5. *You might start by feeling your feet resting on the ground and, after a moment, bring your Attention to your toes. Feel the vibrating response in your fingers and toes simultaneously. You are creating and feeling the edge of your space.*

Awareness

1. *You are defining the edge of your presence, your periphery, with you in the centre. When you are ready, allow that vibrant sensation to lift and flow through your arms and legs and into your whole body.*

2. *As the vibrant sensation flows through the body, your Attention flows through the nervous system, and from simply holding on to four points of contact, your Attention morphs and expands, meeting a space of Awareness.*

3. *You are building that space of Awareness with you in the centre. It is growing from the inside out. You can feel it. Just be there. Feel it grow as you stay present. Stay there.*

4. *And every now and then, allow yourself to be open to this subtle but amazingly real response from the mind-body field. That sense of Awareness, of being here. And it's spacious.*

5. *After a while, your sensing body and thinking mind begin to fall into the background. Any notions of you as a separate, isolated physical and mental thing with worries and concerns begin to fall away. You exist as pure spatial Awareness. You are dimensionless. Edges and boundaries evaporate. There is no inside, there is no outside, there is no past, there is no future, there is no you, there is no me – there just is! An unlimited space of pure Awareness. Absolute consciousness. Feel it! Stay with it.*

Attitude

1. *As you begin to know and rest inside this space, you will notice that it is full of flowing experiences. All is just flowing in-formation. Everything is raw data arising and falling through your space of consciousness.*

2. *Your breath is soft and shallow, with no effort. The space of your body is deeply relaxed and fluid. No effort. The body is breathing for you. The body is sensing for you, feeling for you, sitting for you.*

3. *You still feel the touchpoints. You are still here, sitting on the chair. You still hear and see the mind chatter of thoughts. Your connection to the body and your mind, it has changed. It's all passing. It's all surface. None of it is you.*

4. *You observe that there is something deeper and more fundamental underneath it all. A deeper sense of presence. A witness and observer of everything that is happening. It's YOU. You are not breathing. Your body is breathing for you; it knows what to do.*

5. *Just be with the experience as it is. There is nothing else to do; nowhere else to be – apart from this one-ness. It is growing and unfolding.*

6. *Notice fleeting thoughts as they come and fall away. They come and fall away. They don't concern you. They are not you. You are here.*

7. *Stay with it. You are not trying to change anything. Just watch. You are sitting in space, watching yourself. Just observe that for a few moments.*

8. *Allow yourself to be here. Your Attention is shifting and expanding. You are the observer, watching your mind–body in space. Just watch.*

Action

1. *While you are here. You may notice other things. You are deeply relaxed. This space is real; it has qualities. You can rest in it. And it feels right! You are here, immersed in your present.*

2. *That sense of self is dissolving. Replaced with something more knowing. A feeling of expansion and momentum grows. There is a purpose. There is intention. There is love. There is wholeness. There is connection. You seem to know what to do. No effort. Just know. It may feel deeply familiar; that is because it is. That space is you. And it is good.*

3. *Just observe that for a few moments. Feel your way around it with curiosity. Just know.*

4. *In a few moments, you'll come out of your practice. Remember to keep your eyes closed until it feels right to open them.*

5. *Before that, gently flex your fingers and toes as you work yourself back into the sitting body. Take a little stretch if you want and roll your shoulders back. And gently come back.*

6. *Try not to look at anything straight away. Before moving and leaving your meditation spot, be still and only move when you feel ready to come back into the Doing field of Action.*

Plan to do this twice a day as a formal practice. Work up to 15–20 minutes for both sittings. As you enrich your perception and enhance your neural network and nervous system, it will get easier and more rewarding. After a while, you will find a space you can inhabit anytime, anywhere in your day-to-day world. After a while, you don't need words or guidance. It will happen when you set your intention and switch it on. That's when you start to make real progress and operate in the world from a place of real wisdom and insight. You will know what to do, as solutions come easily for those with a clear and untroubled mind.

Preparing for Informal Practice: Tracking Your Day

Meditation means *to attend*. It means paying Attention to the whole of life as it's happening. It should be effortless, not forced so that the whole of life can be a meditation. There is no need to make dramatic resolutions; just make it your intention to practice experimental self-observation.

What you have to do now is apply what you have learned in your formal practice to the thing you are doing anytime, anywhere. This means learning to separately watch the operation of each of the four 'A's and observing the interplay of these aspects as you go about your day. I have prepared a tracker below to help you do this. This is not an intellectual analysis but a felt learning through the direct experience of self-observation. It means consciously observing one's Actions, speech, thoughts and events. Remember, all Actions and speech, including your gestures and movements, are driven by adaptive unconsciousness, shaped and modified by thought processes. Paying Attention this way, making the unconscious conscious, is key to meditation.

You can use your tracker to do this anytime during the day, or you can pick a time to reflect on a particular event, Action, mindset or speech that may have led you to the centre or to the edge of your tracker. You can even use your tracker to remind you to stay present and flow or as a ready-made journal to record in shorthand how you are doing.

The point of the tracker is to help you stay vigilant and engaged. It acts as a reminder. The goal is **self-actualisation – or conscious Action** every moment, every day, everywhere.

Using the Modern Meditation Tracker

You will recognise the two main axes, the vertical *Being, defined by Attention and Awareness* and the horizontal *Doing, defined by Attitude and Action*. Remember these are your Perception and Processing continua.

Each arm of the axes is divided into nine sections, with the outer edge being 1 and the centre being 9. Your ideal is to try and balance the score on each axis and move inwards towards the centre. In other words, the closer you are to the periphery, the more **unconscious** and **reactive** you have been. The closer to the centre is where you learn to open up and direct your Attention and flow, undertaking **Conscious Action**. Remember, this is the point where life is YOU! You are **whole**, participating in **wholeness**.

You are **whole**, participating in **wholeness**.

This is a *felt* experience, not an exact measurement. It's a device to externalise, record and know on paper. Use your new Modern

Meditation-based skills and treat everything as– formation, as a pointer or message. And be honest with yourself. Work on these skills every day, and record how you are doing using the tracker. Try if you can make them all work together to create and track a smooth regular shape, which over time will encompass the centre.

Example: Emma's Day at Work
Here is Modern Meditation student Emma reflecting on her day at work. She has used the tracker and scored her degree of Conscious Action.

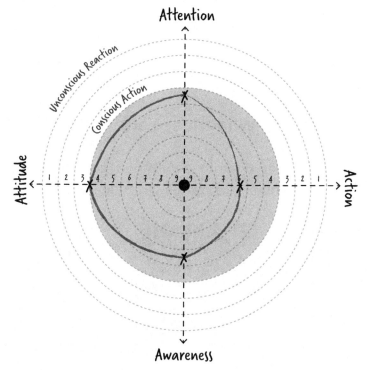

Figure 23: Example tracker – Emma's day at work.

Emma's score
Attention: 4   Awareness: 5   Attitude: 3   Action: 6

From the shape, we can see Emma has had a generally good day managing to stay in a conscious, active space with a good sense of self-awareness and positive action. Her Attitude is just on the boundary between reaction and action, which suggests there were times when she caught herself being distracted or slipping into periods where her Default Mode Network of unconscious reaction happened with her noticing. This might also explain her score on the Attention axes too. The good thing she has **'noticed' and made it conscious.** That is what the tracker is for.

There is no right or wrong here. This is a snapshot, a momentary reflection, a cross-section of Emma's Modern Meditation journey.

There is no right or wrong here.

Informal Practice – What Does Your Tracker Tell You?

To get started you can download your own **beanddo** Modern Meditation tracker by scanning the QR code here:

Reflect on the four A's and select an activity or a moment to track or record. It might be a snapshot of a whole day, a particular experience at work, with friends or family or alone.

Mark your score below against each of the four A skills:

ATTENTION: Today, I have been able to create moments where my Attention has been fully directed towards where I am, who I am with, and what I'm doing.

never		seldom		sometimes		often		always
1	2	3	4	5	6	7	8	9

AWARENESS: Today, I have been able to create moments where I felt fully present, connected and purposeful, inside and out, shaped by the simple joy of being

never		seldom		sometimes		often		always
1	2	3	4	5	6	7	8	9

ATTITUDE: Today, I have created moments where I simply let go and observe all experiences without interference or expectation.

never		seldom		sometimes		often		always
1	2	3	4	5	6	7	8	9

ACTION: Today, I have been able to create moments where I felt completely at one with the task at hand and where I experienced the flowing joy of Doing.

never		seldom		sometimes		often		always
1	2	3	4	5	6	7	8	9

Now mark your scores on the tracker and simply join the dots. You can either draw a smooth curve or a straight line, just as long as you have a shape you can see. Now reflect on the shape you have marked on your tracker. Does it appear balanced or unbalanced? Does it look more like a splat than a reasonably even shape? Is more work required on one or more of the axes? You might need to work a little more on your attitudinal shift or perhaps the quality and application of your Attention. There is no good or bad here. No getting it wrong. Every insight and every experience are important. You are heading in the right direction just by carrying out this exercise.

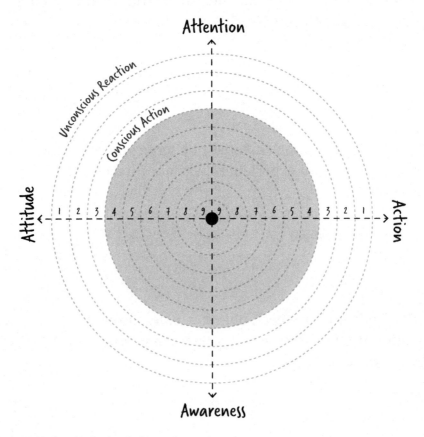

Figure 24: Modern Meditation Daily practice tracker.

Getting a Bit More Reflective

Now study your shape closely and reflect below some key factors that may have determined your score and the shape you have drawn. You might want to draw a version of this chart in your journal.

Conscious ACTION	Unconscious REACTION
Actions, speech or thoughts which lead me towards a more balanced sense of centre: I need to do more of these:	Actions, speech or thoughts which lead me away from a more balanced sense of centre: I need to do less of these:
1.	1.
2.	2.
3.	3.
4.	4.
5.	5.
6.	6.
7.	7.

In the Conscious Action column, you'll probably list moments where you have felt happy, creative, purposeful, balanced, in control, and in flow. In the Unconscious Reaction column, you will most likely list some of the negative habits and reactions you recognised as useless to you on your journey.

By increasingly taking charge and switching to a more conscious life, you will notice how you use your Attention and, thus, your personal energy. With practice, you will increasingly focus on doing what is in the left column. You gradually watch that in the right column weaken and fade away.

Like any good creative, life–changing project, it will take time. But if you are open, honest and willing to try it, you will discover positive change will happen for you as you need it. If you want to live a life which is more meaningful, purposeful, creative and one that puts you right in the heart of your own life flow, then let's start right here, right now.

Affirmation

I am in the Now.
I am the NOW.

See the Inferno

'The first is easy for many: accept the inferno and become such a part of it that you can no longer see it. The second is risky and demands constant vigilance and apprehension: seek and learn to recognize who and what, in the midst of inferno, are not inferno, then make them endure, give them space.'

Italo Calvino

Hopefully, you can see who you thought you were or what others tried to define you as are not real. Until now, your world has been an ever-changing matrix of concepts, images, sensations, assumptions, desires and beliefs that have taken root over time in the mind–body, played unconsciously in the doing field. Some of these constructs that you once *thought* essential to you as a living, breathing individual are actually the very things that seem to be *holding you back*. I see this realisation, this waking up in our students often. The world isn't what they thought it was – literally! So now you have an option. And this insight takes us back to that first question. **Are you created, or are you creating?** Hopefully, you can now see the answer.

With practice, you learn not only to stand back and observe the inner mental commentary about life and the daily experiences encountered. You will also begin to stand back and see a bigger 'story' about who and what you ultimately are, free from the *inferno*. With practice, a shift is created from evaluating thoughts as personal and thus real and who you are to seeing thoughts as impersonal and part of the passing cinema show. You become the audience, but paradoxically, also the actor, writer, designer and director, as well as the screen and projector too. The light, however, is the source of it all, and if it's dimmed the colour and texture of the world and you as the experiencer and collaborator are diminished.

You and the universe are not divided. There is no need to feel lost, lonely or unconnected. In fact, all thoughts, ideas, and actions are formed as creative potential in this field, expressed in the world through your **Conscious Action**. Think about this observation in 'evolutionary' terms. In the Introduction, I defined the 21st century as a revolution in consciousness. But this time, it's not Darwinian. This time, you have to do the work to evolve. It's imperative now. It's a decision we all need to make, as it takes us back into the ultimate purpose of you, me, and the world.

It's about choice now.

As a matter of urgency, we need to find our own light and shift out of its way to avoid casting any more shadows.

AFTERWORD

Afterword by Professor Fiona Measham

What can we do with Modern Meditation? How can I help?

After reading this book and completing multiple yoga and meditation courses with the author Mick Timpson over the years, the question which springs to my mind is what can I do with Modern Meditation? How can it help me to help others? What is my dharma?

Dharma is a Sanskrit word which has slightly different meanings in different religions like Hinduism, Sikhism and Buddhism and cannot be directly and succinctly translated into English. In Hinduism, dharma is the natural cosmic law underlying social order and it forms the basis of the ancient legal system. For Sikhs, dharma means the path of righteousness or the spiritual practice of seeking truth and seeking to experience the Divine within ourselves. Buddhists see dharma as the universal truth taught by the Buddha and if they follow those teachings they will achieve enlightenment. All have a common strand of meaning in it being about a core and unchanging truth, reality or moral order in the universe.

The eight limbs of yoga create a union between the mind and body, translated literally as yoking together or unifying the physical, emotional and spiritual. Meditation is one of the eight limbs of yoga and through that we learn to 'be' and are able to unite 'being' with 'doing', which helps us to identify and to perform our dharma. This can be illustrated by total immersion in the 'flow' of an activity, whatever it might be, to achieve pure bliss. Thus it is through meditation that we can develop our attention and come to experience a timeless awareness and can access our pure consciousness.

Meditation can be translated literally as to attend, as a method of 'switching on' to reality and to who we really are, rather than switching off or escaping. It is by removing the distractions, preconceptions and expectations that we are able to clear a path to our own inner core and more clearly to see life and our own purpose within it. This is a process of trying to identify and attain dharma.

There is a common thread of a commitment to social justice and striving to remove social injustice that I can trace back to childhood, such as arguing passionately against miscarriages of justice or the death penalty, and my mum saying that I should be a barrister when I grew up. Interestingly, for those inclined to astrology, social justice and equality are seen as key characteristics of us Librans too!

My dharma or purpose in life, therefore, might be in the arena of progressing social justice / addressing social injustice. I say 'might' because it will take me a lifetime to fully recognise what my specific purpose in life is, a) to discover my true self, b) to express my unique talents, and to c) put these into practise in the cause of helping others and serving humanity. Deepak Chopra says the key question to ask ourselves in relation to our dharma is: 'how can I help?' By helping others, therefore, we can experience pure bliss. I think this is my dharma because it has been a common thread throughout my life and because if I won the lottery tomorrow, I would still want to do this. The 'doing' of this would be the common thread throughout my work – whether research, writing, teaching, training or setting up my charity – trying to progress this in some way or another, as best I can with the resources I have and in the context in which I live.

For me, identifying what I can do is also about identifying what I can't do, so the role of 'thinker' is more suited to me than the role of 'leader' because I'm happier to be rebelling against authority than to be the authority figure. For example, most recently, this can be illustrated by the appointment of a CEO to my charity. I set up a pioneering and controversial charity and in my spare time spent 10 years working hard to get the service introduced across the UK, including obtaining a grant for a full time CEO. People asked me why I didn't appoint myself. I love my (day) job as an academic, however, and most definitely did not want to become a CEO! I'm the start-up social entrepreneur, motivated by the challenge of getting something seemingly impossible over the line that will reduce drug-related hospital admissions and deaths, at a time when they were the highest in Europe and the highest on record. The person we appointed as CEO has over 25 years' experience in the charity and social care sector and has been very competently running the charity on a day to day basis since her appointment. She has the operational leadership qualities to develop and deliver a national service across the UK, skills which in all honesty I lack and don't have an interest in spending time developing. The last 8 months have been about handing over the reins and not clinging on with founder syndrome, and watching the CEO in action has confirmed that my dharma does not lie in that direction!

When do I experience the 'flow' then? It would be in the passion of persuasion, in a lecture or workshop, or even more so, in a meeting with obstructive policy makers or stakeholders. I hope to bring some of that to meditation instruction in prison and in universities (with my course for architects and artists starting this autumn). In the meantime I will be continuing to apply the art of persuasion in relation to the snail's pace stakeholder negotiations and have started delivering bite-sized free morning mini Modern Meditations to family and friends online. This allows me to practice my patter and pace, to support those who are experiencing anxiety or stress, and to be 'doing' what I love.

Fiona Measham
Chair in Criminology

beanddo trained Modern Meditation Coach and Yoga Teacher

Founder of The Loop (UK 2012, Australia 2018)

BIBLIOGRAPHY

Angelo, W. A Conversation with Professor David Bohm 1990, Beyond Limits; https://bohmkrishnamurti.com/

Aurelius. M. Meditations. Book 4, translated by Robin Hard. Oxford World Classics, 2011.

Bergqvist, A. 'Psychiatric Ethics'. In The Murdochian Mind, ed. Silvia Caprioglio Panizza & Mark Hopwood. London: Routledge, 2022.

Bergqvist, A. 'Companions in Love: Attunement in the Condition of Moral Realism'. In R. Rowland and C. Cowie (eds.), Companions in Guilt Arguments in Metaethics. London: Routledge, 2019.

Bergqvist, A. 'Moral Perception and Relational Self-Cultivation: Reassessing Attunement as a Virtue'. In S. Werkhoven and M. Dennis (eds.), Ethics and Self-Cultivation: Historical and Contemporary Perspectives. London: Routledge, 2018; 197–221.

Blake, W. Songs of Innocence and Experience. Tate Publishing, 1793

Bohm, D. Wholeness and the Implicate Order. Routledge Classics, 1980

Brewer, J.A., et al. 'Meditation experience is associated with differences in default mode network activity and connectivity', Proc Natl Acad Sci U S A, 13 Dec 2011;108(50):20254-9. doi: 10.1073/pnas.1112029108. Epub 2011 Nov 23. PMID: 22114193; PMCID: PMC3250176

Calvino, I. Invisible Cities. Vintage, 1972.

Cohen, L. 'Anthem'. SONY/ATV SONGS LLC, 1992.

Crombie, D & Jardine, C. The Best Alan Watts Quotes. Crombie Jardine, 2016.

Dewey, J. Experience and Education. New York: Macmillan, 1938.

Eliot, T.S. The Four Quartets. Faber and Faber, 1943.

Goldie, P. The Mess Inside. Oxford: Oxford University Press, 2012.

Garrison K.A., et al. 'Meditation leads to reduced default mode network activity beyond an active task', Cogn Affect Behav Neurosci, Sep 2015;15(3):712-20. doi: 10.3758/s13415-015-0358-3. PMID: 25904238; PMCID: PMC4529365.

Gallagher, S., Zahavi, D. The Phenomenological Mind. New York: Routledge, 2012

Gehry, F. Parametric Architecture https://parametric-architecture. com/10-significant-and-inspiring-architectural-projects-of-frank-gehry/]

Gibson. W. (2011). Neuromancer. Oxford World Classics, 2011.

Hawley, J. The Bhagavad Gita. A Walkthrough for Westerners. New World Library, 2001.

Huxley, A. The Divine Within. Selected Writing on Enlightenment. Ed. Jaquelin Hazard Bridgeman, Harper Perennial, 1992.

Kabat-Zinn, J. Wherever You Go, There You Are. London: Piatkus Books Ltd, 1994.

Kafka. F. The Zürau Aphorisms. Published posthumously by Max Brod, 1931.

Kolb, D. 'Experiential Learning: Experience as The Source of Learning and Development'. 1984: https://www.researchgate.net/publication/235701029_Experiential_Learning_Experience_As_The_Source_Of_Learning_And_Development/citation/download

Krishnamurti, J. 'About Core Teachings', https://www.jkrishnamurti. org/about-core-teachings

Kruger, J., & Dunning, D. 'Unskilled and unaware of it: How difficulties in recognizing one's own incompetence lead to inflated self-assessments.' Journal of Personality and Social Psychology, 1999; 77(6), 1121–1134

Lambirth, A. 'Interview with John Hoyland with critic Andrew Lambirth in 2008 interview. http://www.johnhoyland.com/paintings-other-work/

LeGuin, U. quoted by Maria Popova in 'Subjectifying the Universe: Ursula K. Le Guin on Science and Poetry as Complementary Modes of Comprehending and Tending to the Natural World', https://www. themarginalian.org/2018/04/10/ursula-k-le-guin-late-in-the-day-science-poetry/

Lynch, D. Catching the Big Fish: Meditation, Consciousness and Creativity. Michael Joseph, 2007.

Lynch, D. Catching the Big Fish: Meditation, Consciousness and Creativity, 10th Anniversary Edition. New York: Penguin Random House (tarcherperigee), 2006.

ACKNOWLEDGEMENTS

ACKNOWLEDGEMENTS

I am indebted to my editor Sandy who got the idea behind this work quickly. It's well known that dyslexia is common in architects. A superpower for creating and making new spaces, but a real obstacle for writing a book. Thank you, Sandy.

A big thanks goes to Hannah for her wonderful graphic design.

As always, I continue to be overwhelmed by the students I work with. First, thanks to Rebecca for going beyond the call and testing Modern Meditation techniques while running in the Manchester Marathon. Becs has taken my teaching and techniques and made huge changes in her life. Thank you to Amelia for sharing her insight on how and why Modern Meditation worked for her. Her journey too has been extraordinary. And to Pippa who through her creative and personal coaching work has shown how this teaching can make a real difference to both teacher and student.

I am particularly grateful to my long-term friend, student and fellow traveller Mary for introducing me to David Kolb's Learning Styles & Experiential Learning Cycle pedagogy teaching, which my Modern Meditation methodology diagrams are based on. Kolb's work on how one learns in the world has been a game changer for how I teach Modern Meditation.

And finally a huge thank you to Sue who not only managed the building of our new house in Somerset but at the same time made sure that I kept focused and inspired to complete A Modern Way to Meditate. None of this stuff happens without her.

About the Author

Michael Timpson is an architect, artist, author, teacher and modern yoga and meditation coach. He has been teaching yoga and meditation for over 30 years. **A Modern Way to Meditate** follows his first book, Making Happy Work. A beginner's guide to navigating the modern world.

Mick runs yoga and meditation teacher training programmes, coaching, workshops, classes and events through his coaching initiative **beanddo**™. He works 1-2-1, as well as with groups and organisations. He regularly talks at events on the impact of what he calls 'Conscious Action', where individuals discover the joy of Being who they are, and what they can really Do.

www.**beanddo**.co.uk
www.**beanddo**.teachable.com
www.micktimpson.com

Printed in Great Britain
by Amazon

37989719R00145